D0209184

ANOTHER
INSANE
DEVOTION

ANOTHER INSANE DEVOTION

On the Love of Cats
<small>AND</small> *Persons*

Peter Trachtenberg

DA CAPO PRESS
A MEMBER OF THE PERSEUS BOOKS GROUP

Design and production by Linda Mark

Cataloging-in-Publication data for this book is available from the Library of Congress.

First Da Capo Press edition 2012

ISBN 978-0-7382-1526-6 (hardcover)
ISBN 978-0-7382-1617-1 (e-book)

Published by Da Capo Press
A Member of the Perseus Books Group
www.dacapopress.com

Da Capo Press books are available at special discounts for bulk purchases in the U.S. by corporations, institutions, and other organizations. For more information, please contact the Special Markets Department at the Perseus Books Group, 2300 Chestnut Street, Suite 200, Philadelphia, PA, 19103, or call (800) 810-4145, ext. 5000, or e-mail special.markets@perseusbooks.com.

10 9 8 7 6 5 4 3 2 1

To my teachers

ANOTHER INSANE DEVOTION

This was gruesome—fighting over a ham sandwich
with one of the tiny cats of Rome, he leaped
on my arm and half hung on to the food and half
hung on to my shirt and coat. I tore it apart
and let him have his portion, I think I lifted him
down, sandwich and all, on the sidewalk and sat
with my own sandwich beside him, maybe I petted
his bony head and felt him shiver. I have
told this story over and over; some things
root in the mind; his boldness, of course, was frightening
and unexpected—his stubbornness—though hunger
drove him mad. It was the breaking of boundaries,
the sudden invasion, but not only that, it was
the sharing of food and the sharing of space; he didn't
run into an alley or into a cellar,
he sat beside me, eating, and I didn't run
into a trattoria, say, shaking,
with food on my lips and blood on my cheek, sobbing;
but not only that, I had gone there to eat
and wait for someone. I had maybe an hour
before she would come and I was full of hope
and excitement. I have resisted for years
interpreting this, but now I think I was given
a clue, or I was giving myself a clue,
across the street from the glass sandwich shop.
That was my last night with her, the next day
I would leave on the train for Paris and she would
meet her husband. Thirty-five years ago
I ate my sandwich and moaned in her arms, we were
dying together; we never met again
although she was pregnant when I left her—I have
a daughter or son somewhere, darling grandchildren

in Norwich, Connecticut, or Canton, Ohio.
Every five years I think about her again
and plan on looking her up. The last time
I was sitting in New Brunswick, New Jersey,
and heard that her husband was teaching at Princeton,
if she was still married, or still alive, and tried
calling. I went that far. We lived
in Florence and Rome. We rowed in the bay of Naples
and floated, naked, on the boards. I started
to think of her again today. I still
am horrified by the cat's hunger. I still
am puzzled by the connection. This is another
insane devotion, there must be hundreds, although
it isn't just that, there is no pain, and the thought
is fleeting and sweet. I think it's my own dumb boyhood,
walking around with Slavic cheeks and burning
stupid eyes. I think I gave the cat
half of my sandwich to buy my life, I think
I broke it in half as a decent sacrifice.
It was this I bought, the red coleus,
the split rocking chair, the silk lampshade.
Happiness. I watched him with pleasure.
I bought memory. I could have lost it.
How crazy it sounds. His face twisted with cunning.
The wind blowing through his hair. His jaws working.

—Gerald Stern

"Mrkgnao! the cat cried.
They call them stupid. They understand what we say better
than we understand them. She understands all she wants to."
—James Joyce, *Ulysses*

"We know too little of the nature of love to be able to
arrive at any definitive conclusions here."
—Freud, "Notes upon a Case of Obsessional Neurosis"

PREFATORY NOTE

THIS IS A WORK OF NONFICTION. THE CHARACTERS IN IT are based on real people; the events recounted in it actually took place. Still, the facts in this book vary in their density, some being corroborated by documents and interviews and others being drawn from my memory alone. I've tried to make clear which kind of fact is which. The book also contains an artifact, an incident or detail that originates solely in my imagination. I have included it both for aesthetic reasons and out of curiosity about the nature of nonfiction and its tolerance for admixture or adulteration. Nobody doubts that a novel that contains facts—*War and Peace*, for instance—remains a work of fiction. Is the reverse true of nonfiction, and if not, why not? The first reader who identifies the artifact correctly will receive a prize. Originally, I wanted this to be a kitten, but it raised too many questions as to how potential prizewinners would be vetted to weed out psychopaths and the incompetent. At this writing, I'm still looking for a satisfying replacement. Not many things are better than a kitten.

Peter Trachtenberg

1

I FIRST SAW HER A WEEK OR TWO AFTER SOME FRIENDS had rescued her from the woods across from their house, a small, matted thing hunched miserably on a tree branch in the rain while their dogs milled and snapped below. She was very sick with a respiratory infection, and for a while they didn't think she'd make it. By the time I came over to the barn where they were keeping her, she was stronger, but her face was still black with caked-on snot. I sat down on the floor beside her, and the little ginger cat rubbed against me and a moment later clasped my hand between her forepaws and began licking it. It wasn't the grateful licking of a dog; it was proprietary and businesslike, the rasp of her tongue almost painful. She was claiming me.

F. and I named her Biscuit after the color of her fur. She never completely got over the respiratory infection. Even in total darkness, you could tell she'd entered the room because of the snuffling, a sound like a small whisk broom briskly sweeping.

Every few months she'd start sneezing with increasing viscid productivity until it got so gross we had to take her to the vet, which she didn't mind—she'd stroll into her carrier as if it were the first-class compartment of an airliner—and put her on antibiotics, which she did. She hated being pilled and would buck and spit and slash until you got the message. You can see the scars she left on my forearm. Once, when we were still living in the village, Biscuit wandered into a neighbor's garage and came back with half her muzzle and one forepaw white with paint. Three people had to hold her down while a fourth shaved off the painted-on fur so she wouldn't be poisoned while trying to clean herself. It was the angriest I ever saw her. But only a few hours later, she slid into bed with us, snuffling and purring.

This was our marriage bed, my wife's and mine. In it, we had made love; we had quarreled; we had exchanged secrets the way children exchange trading cards. (When I was a kid, these were mostly of baseball players, but there are now cards for WWF Superstars, *Star Wars* characters, and the members of England's royal wedding. Wilfredo, the boy who used to visit us in the summer, had decks of Japanese anime figures.) We had sat up reading by lamplight while the world slept, sometimes silently, sometimes aloud to each other. During the early years of our marriage, the books we read included *Charlotte's Web, Oliver Twist, The Story of the Treasure Seekers*, and the entire *Lord of the Rings*, which aged us like grief. We did the voices of all the characters: guileless, bumptious Wilbur; manly Oswald, bluff as a little Winston Churchill; Templeton rubbing his hands—or I guess his paws—together in anticipation of an all-you-can-eat buffet of purulent midway garbage; unctuous Fagin, his ill will barely concealed by a facade of mocking courtliness; hissing, sniveling Gollum.

Lately we don't read to each other much.

On September 29, 2008, while I was away teaching at a college in North Carolina, I learned that Biscuit had gone missing from our house in upstate New York. F. was also away at the time, at an artists' residency in Europe, so if anybody was going to look for our cat, it would have to be me. By rights, the kid we'd hired to take care of our pets should have gone looking for her, but he was useless—at least, he was useless as a cat-sitter. And so I booked a flight to New York and set off to find Biscuit, though I couldn't afford the airfare and worried that by the time I arrived it would be too late. She'd already been gone three days, a piece of information Bruno the cat-sitter had held back until fairly late in our conversation, I don't know whether from caginess or because it had just slipped his mind.

It was early evening when he called; I was making dinner. I remember looking out the window into the garden of my rental house, which lay in the shadow of the live oak whose acorns, bigger and flatter than the ones I was used to seeing up north, littered the grass like woody bottle caps. It may have been the shade or an approaching storm that gave the dusk a greenish cast. It was like being at the bottom of a well.

"What's the name of your orange cat?" Bruno asked. I felt a surge of anger. He couldn't remember the name of a creature that had been sharing his home—whose home he'd been sharing—for two weeks, a creature whose color was not orange but golden; F. sometimes called her "the golden kitty." But I just told him, "Biscuit, her name's Biscuit. Because she's biscuit colored." In much the same way, parents of missing children describe the clothes they were wearing, their birthmarks, the gaps between their teeth. I know that a child is a child and a cat is just a cat. I'm only trying to say I'm one of those people who greet bad news politely, as if by doing that I could turn it away.

A little over a year before we got Biscuit, my cat Bitey had died. She was the first cat I'd ever owned or owned for more than a few months, a smoke-black domestic shorthair with an underbite that gave her a look of implacable, scheming malice, like Lawrence Olivier playing Richard III. When F. and I moved in together, back when we were still girlfriend and boyfriend, Bitey took an instant dislike to Tina, the younger and more timid of F.'s two cats. Scarcely had we let them out of their carriers than Bitey slipped out of the room where we'd stowed her and shot down the hall into the room where we were keeping Tina. She must have smelled her in passing. Shrieks rent the air. (If any shriek can be said to rend the air, it is a cat's. The shrieks of all other creatures only perturb it a little.) We separated them; that is, we drove Bitey away from the bed under which Tina was cowering, but from then on she spent much of her time lurking outside what we came to call Tina's room, waiting for the little orange cat to tiptoe out—and she really would tiptoe, lifting her paws very high and placing them down as if stepping onto the wrinkled surface of a barely frozen puddle—so she could menace her with her wicked Plantagenet jaw.

Some of this aggressiveness had been apparent even when I adopted Bitey from the Baltimore ASPCA on a wet day in April twelve years before; I remember the statue of St. Francis in the shelter's garden shining with rain. She was just a kitten, barely larger than my fist, and so black she seemed featureless except for her green eyes. My girlfriend held her to her breast as I drove home. D. had a cat of her own that she could handle like a slab of bread dough, but before we'd gone three miles the kitten had squirmed out of her grasp and was pacing along the backs of the seats, mewing. D. tried to pull her down, but she clambered on top of my head and sank her claws into my scalp. She meant no harm by it. Still, her claws were sharp, and I cried out in pain. The black kitten continued to cry out in whatever it was she was feeling: fear, probably, and misery at being shut up in a hurtling cage without her brothers and sisters in it, just two large humans rank with sex and tobacco, toothpaste, deodorant, and shampoo, their mouths brutal with teeth, their nostrils like caves.

A week or so later, after she'd gotten used to me, I had some friends over for dinner. She pranced fearlessly from one to the other, making warlike feints at their hands. My friend Charlie wagged his finger at her, and she nipped it. "Wow! That's a bitey cat you got there!" he said. Up until then I'd been calling her Bridget, but the new name fit her better.

At the time I got Bitey, I had recently entered a new phase of my life. I thought a cat would be part of it, a bolt on the door

I'd shut on all the misdealing and unhappiness that had gone before. A cat would force me to be regular in my habits. It would force me to consider desires other than my own, which up until then had been my main, maybe my exclusive, subject of interest.

I'd had other cats before this, but only in the sense that the singer of "Norwegian Wood" once had a girl. They were cats I found on the street or in apartment buildings and kept for a while, feeding them more or less regularly, cleaning their boxes, but then got tired of or, more to the point, overwhelmed by, and passed on to other caretakers. There was the one who began crying like a rooster at first light, which was only two or three hours after I'd gone to bed: she didn't last too long. There was the silent gray male who scratched my girlfriend T. while she slept. There was the orange female I named Jasmine, who once awakened me from a long nod with an ominous scraping (I thought someone was trying to break into my fourth-floor apartment) that turned out to be the sound of her empty food dish being pushed—butted, really—all the way from the kitchen to the bedroom. I'd liked those cats all right, until they got to be too irritating. I didn't think of them much afterward, except maybe for Jasmine, who one night while I was out pushed aside a window screen and then in all likelihood leaped to a neighboring rooftop, or maybe onto the towering ailanthus in the courtyard, whose branches reached almost to my floor and from there flowed to the ground and melted into the dark. Wherever she went, I hope she found an owner who paid more attention to her and fed her when he was supposed to.

From the very first, Bitey interested me in ways her prede-
cessors hadn't. She was an entertaining presence. For one
thing, she fetched, preferring the crumpled cellophane wrap-
pers of cigarette packets to all the toys I used to buy her in the
pet aisle of the supermarket. Maybe the crackling reminded
her of small animals stirring in the brush. She could hear the
sound anywhere in the house and would come trotting up to
me whenever I opened a fresh pack, her tail twitching with
eagerness. Unlike a dog, she wouldn't drop the cellophane in
your lap or even at your feet, but always far enough away that
you'd have to get up to retrieve it. I don't know if this was out of
the same caution that makes a cat reluctant to eat from a human hand or because, having scrambled around the room in
pursuit of her prize, swatting it from paw to paw, levering it
with surgical dexterity from under a baseboard, lofting it into
the air then showily leaping after it, caroming off walls and
vaulting over the furniture or skidding under it like a toboggan-
ist before finally seizing the ball in her mouth, she wanted me
to get off my ass too.

Most intelligent animals seem to want to be entertained.
This desire may be one of the constitutive features of embod-
ied intelligence, a boundary that separates higher animals from
lower ones and intelligent animals from intelligent machines.
To date we've seen no evidence that computers get bored, not
even the really big ones, designed to measure the expansion of
the universe or track the firefly motion of leptons, that take up
entire multistory buildings. By this standard, the crowning
achievement of our species may not be writing or the pyra-
mids or the cathedral at Chartres—all of which, face it, can be

boring—but *Grand Theft Auto*. I'm not sure if it would be possible to make a cat understand what writing is for. (Maybe if you could somehow demonstrate that it was our way of rubbing ourselves against the furniture or, alternatively, of spraying). But I can imagine a cat staring raptly at *Grand Theft Auto*, especially on a big screen.

When Bitey chased a ball of crumpled cellophane, as Biscuit chased cloth balls stuffed with catnip, she may simply have been practicing the behaviors she'd need for hunting. But I think she was also engaged in something gratuitous and nonutilitarian that might be called fun. A 1954 study found that even "Kaspar Hauser" cats, cats "reared in social isolation and without opportunities for visual experience, let alone play behavior," displayed normal predatory responses when presented with a "prey-like" moving dummy. (Leave aside the ethical implications of raising a young social animal in what amounts to solitary confinement and—judging by the experimenter's offhand "without opportunities for visual experience"—total darkness.) From my own observation, I know that Bitey would go scrambling after a tossed projectile moments after she'd finished eating, often with such abandon that she vomited in mid-pursuit. Her vomiting was brisk and without fanfare. Suddenly she'd brake; her body would be seized by spasms that squeezed and stretched it like a concertina. These would be accompanied by gasps of esophageal exertion, though "gasps" leaves out the sound's distinctive Elvis Presleyan glottal stop. It was purely functional, without the notes of outrage and self-loathing that characterize human retching, whose sound is always the sound of someone groaning, "Why? Why? Why?" in a filthy bathroom at midnight. Bitey didn't wonder why. What had gone into her was now making its way out. When it came, she looked at it blandly, then shook her head and walked away.

My girlfriend D. had a dramatic personality. She wore her hair dyed platinum blonde and swept back from her forehead like a romantic composer's. She played the keyboards at three in the morning. She would fix you with hypnotic stares of desire or grief, her pupils big as jelly beans, waiting for you to jump her or apologize for the terrible thing you'd done to her. When she smiled, her mouth was shaped exactly like an upside-down boomerang. The night we met, she watched me pour a bottle of wine down the kitchen sink; I think it was a Beaujolais nouveau. The first time we made love was also marked by ceremony. We'd put off the moment for a while. I'd never delayed gratification of any kind before, just had it delayed for, or do I mean from, me, dangled out of reach like a catnip toy, and I have to say that when you're the one who does the dangling, it drives the other person crazy. It drives *you* crazy. Like the old ascetics of the desert, you're intoxicated by your self-denial, not to mention your unexpected power over another person. Not that this was my reason for postponing sex. It had more to do with the new life that had begun only a day or two before I met D., one event following the other so closely that I thought of them as cause and effect. In my mind, D. was' the reward for my new life, which in its early stages was marked mostly by what it required me to give up, as if I had joined a priesthood whose members dressed in mufti and chain-smoked. Those rooms murky with cigarette smoke. Even in mid-summer, you seemed to be huddling by a fire, trying to make out your comrades' features through the gloom. "I want to wait," I told D., and kissed her the way you kiss someone when that's the only way you have of entering her. When we finally did it, it was the most powerful sex I'd had in my life up till that moment. In an old movie, it would have been symbolized by a shot of water crashing down the flume of a dam or steam surging through a pipe. (With the passing of heavy industry, we are losing an entire category of metaphors for the sexual act, metaphors of vast forces allowed only a single conduit through which to make themselves felt in the world. The turning of cogs and gears, the thrumming of turbines, the entranced pounding of pistons into cylinders: all gone. I suppose new metaphors will arise out of the new technologies, but how much fun can sex be without build or friction, only the whirr of boot-up or the chime of a new message materializing in your in-box?)

With D., I wore my last Halloween costume, suffering miserably with one half of my face painted black and the other painted white. She wasn't the first woman I ever apologized to, but she may have been the first to whom I apologized because I was wrong and felt bad about it rather than just because I wanted to end a fight. I couldn't say what I was apologizing for. My moral proprioception was still coarse back then and could identify only the grosser transgressions: if I'd screwed somebody else, I would've known it was wrong. Still, I remember the remorse rising in me like nausea. Once, when we were fighting in the car while caught in traffic, I made a violent turn that brought one half of the Tercel lurching over the curb for a second before dropping back with a tooth-rattling thud, and

D. accused me of trying to kill her; maybe I was. Once she told me to go and fuck my way around the world if that was what I wanted. On at least two occasions, she told me that she loved me more than air. One of these was at a birthday party, before an audience of aww-ing friends. Even now I remember how my face burned with pleasure and embarrassment. The pleasure was pleasure at being loved, of course, but it was also indicative of my own taste for drama, which in years past had led me to many sad feats of clownish vainglory. The embarrassment suggests that my appetite for drama wasn't what it had been. When you're a little kid, grown-ups warn you that your eyes are bigger than your stomach, but there comes a time when that's no longer true, not because your stomach has gotten bigger but because your eyes have gotten smaller.

"I love you more than air," D. said. I said, "I love you," and immediately felt at a disadvantage, as if I'd followed her inside straight with a pair of eights. Everybody knows that the thing to do then is fold. I did, but it took me several more months. I'm not sure why. One morning I woke up and was no longer in love with her. Then she was gone, and I was left wondering what had happened to everything I'd felt for her, where I'd lost it.

I often think that my relationship with Bitey might have been much different if not for something that happened in the first year I had her. I was alone in the house. It was an early evening in winter; there was a sting in the air. I was suddenly overcome with tiredness—I hadn't been sleeping much since I'd broken up with D.—and lay down on the couch in the dining room, resting my head on a padded arm. Bitey jumped up and settled on my chest. At first she sat gazing down at my face. Then she lay down on top of me and stretched her forelimbs so that she was almost clasping me around the neck and began to purr. We stayed like this for a long time. I could feel her breath on my face. Abruptly, the phone rang, and I started up to answer it, jostling my cat from her place of rest and spilling her onto the floor. She wasn't hurt; she was a cat, and cats routinely fall from much higher up without injury. But she never lay down on me like that again or clasped my neck in what I always insist was an embrace. I'm probably reading too much into that moment. I was lonely, and Bitey may just have been stretching.

We think of love, at least love in its ideal form, as a reciprocal condition, like a current that requires two poles to make one's hair rise; without two poles, you can't even speak of a current. Unreciprocated love may not be love at all, but a delusion, maybe a pathetic delusion, maybe a creepy one. Stalkers, too, think they're in love. Well, if someone says, "I love you," it's nice to be able to say, "I love you," back. This is more difficult than it sounds. In James Salter's *Light Years*, a little girl is writing a picture story: *Margot loved Juan very much, and Juan was mad about her.* But Margot is an elephant, and Juan is a snail. In the classical myths, humans and gods love one-sidedly, a predicament the gods usually solve by means of rape. The poor humans just pine. Tristan and Iseult may be the poster children for requited love, but even they needed a love potion, and it's significant, I think, that the love they came to embody, courtly love, has conditions so extreme as to be essentially unrealizable. It must be adulterous; it must be pure. The lovers must love equally. We have to speak of such love the way we speak of black holes. Who knows what happens to someone who enters a black hole? Is he crushed by its gravity, which is massive enough to crush stars? Do its attractive forces wrench him in two or draw him into a wire of infinite length and infinitesimal thinness and stretch him across all space and time? What message does that wire transmit, and who hears it?

There was a moment when F. and I loved each other equally, when we looked at each other with eyes whose pupils were similarly dilated. F.'s pupils were easier to see because her eyes are blue. Mine are dark, and this makes the state of the pupils more elusive, a trait I found useful back when I was getting high.

There are nights when I wake beside my wife as if beside a stranger. Her body is familiar to me; I know it almost as well as my own. Maybe I know it better, having looked at it and touched it with greater attention than I ever gave myself, because I wanted to know it. There've been few things in my life I've wanted to know so badly. But something's gone wrong. Two years ago, she asked for a separation. A while later she changed her mind. I couldn't tell you why. Or rather, I could tell you: Because of the children we didn't have or the child we borrowed. Because of the kitten we rescued and then lost. Because of money, because of sex. Because I didn't pay enough attention to her, because I paid too much. Because she got bored, and then got interested again. But any of those explanations would be wrong.

Now it's my turn. I don't know what to do with F. I look at her the way you look at a house you are thinking of moving out of. It's gotten too small for you. It needs a new furnace; the floor slants. Why do you stay? But how can you ever leave?

"They lay in the dark like two victims," Salter writes of a husband and wife, "They had nothing to give one another, they were bound by a pure, unexplicable love. . . . If they had been another couple she would have been attracted to them, she would have loved them, even—they were so miserable."

I remember when people still spoke of couples as being estranged. "Miss Taylor and Mr. Burton are estranged." The term has passed out of use—unfortunately, because it is so accurate and absent of blame, saying nothing about which party has become the stranger and leaving implicit the fact that when one falls out of love, as when one falls into it, one becomes a stranger to oneself. Proust describes that earlier estrangement well, when he has Swann realize, with an inward start, that he has fallen in love with Odette, whom only a little while before he found a little boring and her beauty a little worn:

> He was obliged to acknowledge that now, as he sat in that same carriage and drove to Prévost's, he was no longer the

same man, was no longer alone even—that a new person was there beside him, adhering to him, amalgamated with him, a person whom he might, perhaps, be unable to shake off, whom he might have to treat with circumspection, like a master or an illness.

I gaze down at my wife in the dark but see only the dim curve of her body lying on its side like a letter C, a face shuttered in sleep. I go into the bathroom and turn on the light above the sink. My face in the mirror is the face of a tramp rousted from a ditch. I lean closer and try to make out the size of my pupils, but of course the sudden brightness has made them pin. In mechanical terms, there's something they don't want to see. The door creaks; I turn in alarm, but it's only our plush silver tabby Zuni, that fool for running water, shouldering her way inside. She hops expectantly into the sink. I turn on the tap for her; she laps without a glance in my direction, like a duchess so used to being ministered to that she no longer notices the servants and sees only a world where objects dumbly bend to her wishes, doors opening, faucets discharging cool water, delicious things appearing in her dish.

Is it that I don't know F. any more or that I don't know myself? Maybe it's love that has become strange to me. I can't recognize it in another person. I can't find it in myself. It has become my lack. But this seems to be true of many people: of Salter's glamorously wretched married couple; of Swann, trembling at the loss of his faithless mistress, whom he will marry only when he has fallen out of love with her; of all the seekers who crawl and flounder after this one thing, turning over wives, husbands, lovers, mistresses, like rocks in a garden, under one of which, long ago, they buried a treasure. Or maybe just a dream of treasure.

What is this treasure?

It took me about twenty-two hours to travel the 1,400 miles from the town where I was teaching to the mid–Hudson Valley and back. That's one of the drawbacks of flying on a discount carrier. To Biscuit, the distance would be as incomprehensible as that between Earth and the sun, whose warmth she loved to bask in when it poured through the living room window on winter afternoons. Though, come to think of it, you hear stories of cats traveling long distances all the time. Usually, they're trying to return to a former home or be reunited with a missing owner. To me, why Biscuit wandered off and where she went are, if not incomprehensible, unknowable. Still, I can recount just about every step of my search for her and many of the key incidents of our relationship before then.

This is more than I can do for my relationship with F., which at the time Biscuit disappeared was beginning to change and, maybe, to draw to an end; it's still too early to say. I recall that relationship at least as vividly as I do the one with Biscuit, if not more vividly, but, as Freud showed us, there is such a thing as an excess of vividness. The most vivid memories, the ones most populous with detail and saturated with color, may be the least reliable. And my relationship with F. may also be too complex to be easily narrated. Both of us can talk, and that means we can contradict each other. (A cat can defy you, but it can't contradict you, its powers being confined to the realm of action as opposed to the realm of descriptions of action, which belongs to humans.) I feel no obligation to relate F.'s version of the events I lay out here. Still, when her version contradicts mine, I feel haunted. My past seems to belong to someone else, a self I am only impersonating. Did I really do the things I remember doing, say the things I remember saying? And whom did I say them to?

About my cat and the self I am with her, I have fewer doubts.

I turn off the faucet. The silver tabby goes on lapping. I still hear her after I turn off the light, swabbing up the last drops of moisture. I feel my way in the dark to our marriage bed and climb under the blankets beside my wife. In the dark, I listen for the creak of floorboards and the sound of a small whisk broom briskly sweeping.

2

O N SEPTEMBER 29, BRUNO HAD BEEN STAYING IN THE
house for a little more than a week. That was long
enough for me to understand that he didn't return phone calls
with the promptness one values in a cat-sitter. I'd had to leave
four or five messages just to get him to call me back and tell
me wearily—he might've been talking to his mom—that the
cats were fine. So when his name came up on my caller ID a
few days later, before I'd even begun to pester him again, I felt
a twinge of unease, and the moment I heard his voice, my
whole being constricted like a muscle in spasm. He'd let Biscuit out as usual, he told me, and she hadn't come back. I said
nothing. He'd thought she would, since it was raining. It had
been raining almost nonstop. I felt ill. I should never have told
him he could let her out. I should never have let her out at all,
considering what had happened to Gattino a year before. I
asked Bruno how long she'd been gone, and it was his turn to
fall silent. "Was it Sunday?" I wanted to throttle him through

the phone. "Saturday, Saturday morning." Two and a half days. Back when we'd lived in the village, she'd stayed away for as long as three, sustained by the generosity of our neighbors and an abundance of slow-moving mice and voles. I told him to go out and call her. "It's best if you say her name three times." I showed him how F. and I did it; I used a falsetto. It's true that was the voice she most responded to, but I suspect I was also taking some mean pleasure in the thought of this big, preening kid being made to squawk, "Biscuit, Biscuit, Biscuit!" in a mortified falsetto on the back porch of our house, within earshot of a women's college dorm. "Try it now," I told him. "And call me if she comes. Call me if she doesn't come."

~ ~ ~

We brought our new cat into the house the way they always tell you to, sequestering her behind closed doors for a few days so our other cats could get used to her scent and she to theirs, then bringing her out in a carrier, like a visiting dignitary in a covered litter, for a formal presentation. None of it was necessary. It helped that one of our cats was very old and arthritic, and another was old and senile, and Tina, the third, was almost as fearful as she'd been four years before. But most of the credit is Biscuit's. She was so easygoing. When the other cats approached her carrier, she rubbed against the gate and purred. Nobody purred back, but nobody struck at her either, and within a week the new arrival was eating with the older residents and calmly touching noses with them when they met on the stairs.

She had health problems, starting with the copious wet sneezing. A small raised bump on her neck became an open

sore that made you wince with pity and disgust. Biscuit herself
seemed oblivious to it, except for the two times a day when we
daubed the wound with antibiotic ointment. Another cat would
have gone into hiding whenever it saw its owners heading toward it with nonchalant expressions and a tube of Neosporin.
This one stood her ground. She struggled, of course, rearing up
on her hind legs and striking out with her claws, snorting with
anger and congestion. But at some point she let herself be over-
powered and tended to, all the while making it clear how so not
crazy she was about it. Maybe it was because she was still young
and hadn't perfected the tactics that would make her so hard to
medicate later on. I thought of this as being somehow indicative of her character, of its forthrightness and stalwartness. We
don't consider these feline qualities—if anything, you'd call
them canine qualities—but intelligent animals often display
traits that seem alien to their species. Think of those aloof dogs
that don't even prick up an ear when a visitor makes an entrance. Think of horses that stay imperturbable in the midst of
cannon fire. The more intelligent the animal, the more of its
traits will seem uncharacteristic or anomalous, until it becomes
hard to say if any of its traits are characteristic: this may be why
we have so much trouble deciding what is truly human.

Biscuit was still healing when she went into heat. She was
so little that we'd figured she was younger. She'd pace about
the house squalling, the soft furrow below her tail suddenly,
shockingly distended. The transformation of her body seemed
to puzzle her; her cries held a puzzled note. What's happening
to me? What do I want? Why do I want it so bad? Here, too,
I'm projecting. There was nothing for her to be puzzled about.

She had instinct, which is to organisms what gravity is to matter, and so on some level she knew what was going on. Still, the baffled-sounding appeals went on for days. We had to be watchful at the door to keep her from lunging out or a horny male from stealing in. The other cats looked at her strangely. Even our old tom Ching, who was gaunt with hyperthyroidism and addled with dementia and hadn't been interested in sex even when he still had his balls, sniffed at her as she passed and opened his mouth in a Kabuki grin. F. would growl at him, urging him to remember what a tiger he was.

I was fascinated by what was happening to our cat, and especially by the flagrancy of her vulva. It looked so much like a woman's. That was part of the shock of it. Our Biscuit had turned into one of those mythical hybrids like a mermaid or a Minotaur: a little cat with a woman's sex between her legs, her hind ones. My wife has a dark view of sex, or say, a tragic view, and I often imagined how that view might apply to Biscuit. She'd be touched to see our new pet growing up into an adult female who in the natural course of things would mate and bear kittens that she'd ferry proudly around in her mouth. And at the same time, F. would know how cruel the mating could be, the feline penis being barbed and its possessor securing his grip on the female with teeth and claws. And she would know how that cruelty pales beside the cruelty of sex among humans, who being born without barbs on their genitals have to fashion them, the males and the females both. Maybe I'm just speaking of my own view of sex, which is also pretty dark. But we were both relieved when Biscuit went out of heat and we could take her to be spayed.

The first time I thought I might love F.—that is, thought of her as someone I might come to love—was at a tea shop in my old neighborhood in the city. I don't like tea, but F. did, and I suppose the fact that I agreed to meet at a tea shop was a sign that I already wanted to please her. I drank coffee; it was bad. F. took her tea with milk and so much sugar, dumping in spoon after precariously heaped spoon of it, that I could smell the sweetness across the table. If you'd asked me a month before, I would've said that a tea shop would be the last place on earth you'd go to meet her. Her watchful, brittle cool seemed more suited to a dimly lit cocktail lounge with cunningly shaped glassware filled with liquor blue as antifreeze. Over tea, she told me that when she was nine or ten, her family had moved to a new town, where other kids immediately identified her as a goat. Girls made a show of ignoring her as she passed them in the school hallways. Boys called out taunts as she walked home. The worst oppressors were three or four popular girls in her class. They made F. wish she had magic powers. I asked her if she'd wanted them for revenge; I'm sure I sounded eager. She looked offended. "No, not *revenge*—I wasn't that kind of kid. I wanted to conjure up Beatle dolls." She saw my incomprehension. "To give the girls. Those girls were always talking about how they wanted Beatle dolls. Everybody wanted them back then; it was the year of Beatle dolls. And I thought how cool it would be if I had magic powers so I could come up to them and say"—she snapped her fingers—"'Look, Beatle dolls!'"

Her smile had a child's guilelessness. Just so a child might offer you a bouquet of wildflowers she'd picked from the side of the road. I think I mooed, "Oh, that's sweet!" I know I reached for her, meaning to stroke her cheek. She shrank from me. The cool that had receded a little dropped back down like a visor, with an almost audible click. I was too mortified to apologize. It would be like apologizing for farting. We left the tea shop and stood outside in the falling dusk, watching the pavement change color as the traffic light on the corner clicked from red to green. I was sure this was the last time I'd ever see her. "I'm sorry about what happened back there. I didn't mean anything." I waited for her to say, "It's all right."

She said, "I just don't like to be touched like that. I don't know you." Then she left.

Afterward, it seemed to me that I'd been exposed to two completely different personalities. One was magnanimous; the other was grudging. One would repay ostracism with magic Beatle dolls; the other recoiled from a touch. One was deeply attuned to other people's desires; the other was almost oblivious to them, or at least oblivious to the desire for forgiveness of someone who'd committed a minor social error (at least I thought it was minor; it wasn't as if I'd done what a friend of mine, a singer, had once had done to her by a guy she met at one of her gigs. "I really like the way you sing," he'd told her when she sat down with him during the break. "It came right from the clit." And by way of illustration, he reached for it). The alternation between these personalities was so shocking that my automatic response was to label one as the real F. and the other a false self, a facade, a cutout. And for the rest of that night and many nights afterward, I occupied myself trying to figure out which was which. If the true self is the one that's most readily evident to an observer, then the true F. was the watchful, defensive one, her gaze unblinking, her soft features impassive. If the true self is the one that's kept tucked away like a hole card, the true F. was the one who beamed as she gave treasure to traducers.

I know this episode doesn't say much about her. She likes tea, not coffee, or liked it then, with milk and lots of sugar. As a child, she experienced displacement and the cruelty of her peers and responded with generosity, at least in her imagination. (If it had been my imagination, I would've been wiping the floor with those boys and making the girls fall grovelingly in love with me so I could reject them.) She doesn't like strangers touching her. It's all I can say. There's only so much you can say about a wife.

Here a few punch lines suggest themselves:

"I mean to her face."

"Unless she's *your* wife."

"If you want to keep her."

Baddabing.

Marriage accommodates all sorts of betrayals. It is, in a sense, betrayal's dedicated environment, a hot air balloon whose skin is so easily punctured by the pointy accessories of its passengers, a high-heeled shoe, a tiepin, a toothpick. I may not know if I want to keep my wife, but I don't want to betray her, or at least not her privacy, considering that her sense of privacy is essentially what caused her to flinch when I first tried to touch her face. A person is a laminated entity, and the body is only one of its layers. It may not be the most intimate one. There are beaches where people—not even very good-looking people—

promenade on the dunes gaily displaying their genitals like designer purses. There are rooms where strangers proclaim their secrets to each other in voices choked with snot and tears: they pay money for this. The appeal of these practices is the appeal of divestiture, a word that comes from the Latin for "to take off clothing." They're supposed to make you feel lighter, though clothing doesn't weigh very much and secrets weigh nothing at all. In an attempt to combine the two kinds of divestiture, F. and I once imagined a therapeutic retreat where people would strip naked and partner up, with one partner lying on her (or his) back with her (or his) feet clasped in the yoga position known as the "Happy Baby," while the other peered studiously into the body cavities thus exposed with the aid of a flashlight and magnifying glass. "Intimacy," the group leader would croon, "means 'into-me-see.'"

To me the definitive image of nakedness has always been Masaccio's *The Expulsion of Adam and Eve from the Garden of Eden*. The Adam and Eve depicted in it don't look light. Adam's back is bowed. Eve is covering her breasts and sex. She doesn't do this like someone shielding herself from a lustful gaze; she covers them the way one covers a wound. Curiously, Masaccio's Adam doesn't cover his parts but his face, as people do when they weep. Even children do this, from a very young age. I think of these two figures as personifying two kinds of violated privacy, the privacy of the body and the privacy of the soul.

The soul is often thought of as residing in the eyes. "I looked into his eyes and saw his soul," George W. Bush said after meeting the Russian premier. Proust is more long-winded, though his long-windedness is dictated by precision. He calls the eyes "those features in which the flesh becomes a mirror and gives us the illusion that it allows us, more often than through other parts of the body, to approach the soul."

F. and I went to see the *Expulsion* a few years ago in Florence. It was July, a terrible time to be there, so hot we had only to step out of the hotel to feel the air being sucked from our lungs, and verminous with tourists. We were part of that vermin. We walked for many hours, uncomplainingly, down narrow streets, past shops selling gold-stamped leather goods or old maps or ice cream. Every so often we'd enter a square where a crowd milled around a gigantic dome like an ant colony around a fallen sugar bun. The *Expulsion* was located in the Church of Santa Maria del Carmine. It was part of a sequence of frescoes Masaccio had painted in the Brancacci Chapel. A few feet away people were praying. My wife was surprised by that. She

Masaccio, *The Expulsion of Adam and Eve from The Garden of Eden* (1426–1428), Cappella Brancacci, Santa Maria del Carmine. Courtesy of the Granger Collection.

hadn't been in many churches before, and not until she came to Italy had she been in one where the cults of God and art were worshipped side by side with no apparent friction between their adherents. The art viewers stood, talking in (mostly) low voices; the churchgoers sat in silence. We looked at the painting. The bowed figures seemed small, humble, two ordinary humans who, out of a momentary desire, a whim, had tripped the switch of the doomsday machine of sin and death. Adam's body was the body of the laborer he would become, condemned to wrest his food from the earth and eat it salted with sweat and tears. Eve had the spreading hips and drooping breasts of someone who has already borne children. In Genesis this doesn't happen until after the expulsion; the expulsion is the first punishment. But my guess is that Masaccio wanted viewers to see the full consequences of that first act of disobedience, and so he had shown Adam and Eve stumbling out of paradise, shamefaced and weeping, their flesh already marked with their sin.

I turned to point this out to F., but she'd left my side. I found her in one of the pews, sitting with her hands folded in her lap. "What are you doing?" I asked her. She said, "I'm praying." Then she asked, "Do you want to pray with me?" I said yes. I did as well as I was able. The walls of the chapel were pale gray marble or granite; light seemed to dwell beneath their surface. I stole a glance at my wife. She was looking straight ahead, and in profile I could see that her eyes were deeply sunken. That always happens when she's upset. I knew what she was praying for. She was praying for a cat.

~ ~ ~

The first person I called after hanging up on Bruno was Sherri, who usually watched the cats for us when we went away. I felt sheepish, considering that I was asking her for help finding the cat the kid we'd hired in her place had lost. I might have explained that the only reason we'd done that was because at twenty bucks a visit we couldn't afford to hire her for an entire month, but then she could have reminded me that you get what you pay for. However, she was gracious. She doubted Biscuit had gone very far. She was a bright animal who knew where her Friskies were dished out, and she was probably just wandering around the property, sheltering beneath the eaves of the barn when it got too wet. Sherri said she'd come over and help look for her. In the meantime, Bruno should be sure to call Biscuit from different locations on the property, not just from the porch but from the driveway and the front door and the toolshed out back, and leave out a bowl of food to remind her that home was where good things came from. I phoned Bruno to repeat these instructions, but he didn't pick up. Maybe he was still outside, calling, "Biscuit, Biscuit, Biscuit!" in the rain. Maybe he'd turned off his phone.

I don't remember whom else I phoned that evening, only that I mostly stayed in the kitchen, gazing out the window into the yard. Once or twice I stepped out onto the deck to pace until the rain—for it was raining where I was too—forced me back inside. I couldn't stay still, but I didn't want to go anywhere else in the house. It would mean losing sight of the big live oak and the beds of modest, garden-variety flowers and the lawn I clipped with a rickety mechanical push mower whose unamplified whirr was so much more pleasing than the engorged growl of the Sears Craftsman I used up north. I kept the deck lights on. I often saw cats sunning themselves in the yard, and maybe on some unconscious level, I thought that if I waited long enough, I would see Biscuit there too.

~~~

I don't remember Bitey going into heat, only bringing her back from the vet after she'd been spayed. She was so listless I had to scoop her out of the carrier. She rose unsteadily and looked about her, then drank a little water before stumbling off to the spot by the radiator where she liked to sleep. I watched her through the day. Did she always sleep this long? Did her stomach look swollen, or was that just because it was shaved? (The awful nakedness of a cat's shaved stomach!) Shouldn't she be drinking more? I was used to sick people. All through my teens my mother and grandfather took turns trooping in and out of the hospital like the allegorical figures in those clocks you see looming over town squares all over Germany. I once saw one whose automata included Death, gliding out in his black shroud, wielding his scythe with a jerk. But sick people can tell you what's wrong with them, more or less, and what they want. Sick animals can't. You have to read them. You lean over them as you would lean over a book, gauging the rise and fall of their breath, the luffing of a ribcage, a wheeze, a sigh, the twitch of a lip. Of course, Bitey wasn't sick then, just postoperative, and a day later she was eating normally and chasing wads of cellophane around the living room.

She seemed not to miss her uterus, no more than Ching, the stripy male I got to keep her company a year later, seemed to miss his balls after they were snipped off. The night before his procedure, Bitey wrestled him onto his back and began roughly grooming him. (Felinologists call this behavior allogrooming and identify it with dominance. You can spot the top cat in any colony by seeing which one most frequently grooms the others.) At one point it looked as if she was about to lick his genitals, but he pushed her away with his forepaws like someone trying to hold a door shut against the pounding of housebreakers. "Don't stop her, you fool!" I yelled at him. "It's your last chance!" It was no use; it might not have been even if he'd had an inkling of what I was yelling about.

Well, he must have had an inkling. On an average, male cats roam some three times farther than females, and given that both genders need roughly the same amount of food, one assumes it's because the males are looking for sex. This is borne out by a study by Olof Liberg, in which dominant—that is, breeding—male house cats were found to have an average roaming range of 350 to 380 hectares versus 80 for nonbreeding "subordinates." You don't have to travel very far if you're only going out for carton of milk.

Of course, those roaming cats were acting on the same imperative that made Biscuit stalk through the house presenting her swollen genitals for somebody to do something with: they were acting on instinct. What I'd like to know is how they experienced that instinct, whether it was just a blind hormonal goading or was accompanied by thought, or some version of thought. Did those dominant males have an internal schema of sex that summoned them out of their houses, made them cross yards and slink under hedges, skitter up trees, creep into culverts, dart across roads where cars shot past in sprays of dust and exhaust, avid, tireless, pausing only to sniff and twitch their ears? Did they know what they were after? Not in words, I mean, but in pictures—say, the silhouette of a lordotic female—or as an archetypal scent they had been born knowing and whose corporeal traces they kept seeking in the fragrant air?

I have in mind something like the sexual theories of young children, those murky ideas of sticking one part into another part that used to trouble me when I was six or seven, referring as they did to something I already wanted to do without being at all clear as to what it was. The indeterminacy is suggested by the first dirty joke I remember learning. John Wayne meets Marilyn Monroe and asks her, "You want to come to my house?" Marilyn Monroe says, "Sure." They go to his house, and he asks her, "Can I go to bed with you?" and Marilyn Monroe says, "Okay, but don't get any ideas." So John Wayne gets into bed with Marilyn Monroe. "This is nice," he says. "Don't you think it's nice?" Marilyn Monroe says, "It's okay, I guess. But don't get any ideas." Then he asks her, "Can I feel your boobies?" She says, "Sure, but don't get any ideas." So Marilyn Monroe shows John Wayne her boobies, and he feels them with his hands. Then John Wayne says, "Hey, can I put my finger in your belly button?" And Marilyn Monroe says, "Oh, okay, but don't get any ideas." After a while, Marilyn Monroe says, "Hey, that's not my belly button." John Wayne says, "That's okay. That's not my finger."

I heard this joke in my first year of grade school, from the boy sitting at the desk next to mine. I don't remember anything about him, but I can still remember the sweet voltage that tore through me as I got his meaning. "That's not my finger." For a moment, I was almost too shocked to laugh. Then I did, out of the same shock that had struck me dumb a moment before. I can't imagine how I kept it quiet, but I must have, or else Mrs. Mehrer would have been on top of me, wanting to know what was so funny and if I'd like to share it with the other children. This was what the entire world knew. Now I did too.

In the months before F. and I got married, I was unexpectedly haunted by thoughts of the women I would never have sex with. I thought about women I knew and women I walked past on the street or sat across from in the subway, women I glimpsed in movie lines, women who bumped me with their shopping carts in the narrow aisles of the discount gourmet. I'd turn, readying my most ferocious glare, but the moment I saw their eyes burning back at me, it was all I could do not to swoon onto the cheese counter. I was like the teenaged St. Augustine, blinded by "the mists of passion that steamed up," as one translation puts it, "out of the puddly concupiscence of the flesh." But I was in my forties. I pined for women I eavesdropped on in restaurants. How guilty I felt for listening to them! Their fragmentary conversations were so hot. Even their toughness was flirtatious. Their flirting was like a punch in the mouth. "He says, $850, take it or leave it. I say I'll leave it." "Uh oh, you're getting the oysters. Does that mean I'm in trouble?" It drove me crazy. F. could have said the same things, and I would barely have noticed. She's not coy that way, and she wouldn't ask if she was in trouble unless she'd gotten a letter from the IRS.

In the first sentence of the preceding paragraph, the operative word, the word that lends it force, is "never." The women I
would never have sex with. Had any of those women been
available to me—had I been available to them—I doubt I
would have felt much of anything. I could have overheard
them talking about their orgasms. Their charge was the charge
of the forbidden. In an earlier time, I might have spoken of
those women as forbidden fruit, in keeping with the tradition
that links sexual transgression to the prototypical transgression
of the first human beings. A difference is that in Genesis, the
prohibition against eating from the Tree of Knowledge is not
in itself arousing. God warns Adam against eating its fruit, and
Adam doesn't think about it; he's too busy naming the animals.
Not even slutty Eve would have conceived a yen for that fruit if
not for the serpent telling her how delicious it was, and so rich in
antioxidants. Only in the erotic sphere do prohibitions have the
opposite effect, giving their objects the sheen and perfume of
the most wonderful fruit that ever hung from a branch—not the
hackneyed apple, which is so often woody or mushy and whose
hard core gouges the palate, but the grape, as is written in the
Zohar, or the fig, which when split open so resembles a woman's
sex. What you can't have is what you want. Because I knew their
outcome—because I knew they *would have* no outcome—my
encounters—or, more accurately, my sightings—always had an
elegiac quality. It may not have been that different from what
the very ill and the very old feel as they do things for what they
suspect will be the last time: the last time they walk through
the park; the last time they sit beneath a chestnut tree and
watch the sunlight streaming through its leaves; the last cup of

strong coffee; the last time someone they love combs their hair. What I felt for those women wasn't just desire, which by itself may not be enough to make you sag against the cheese counter at the Fairway; it was mourning.

During this time I got an assignment from a tony sex magazine to write a story about a woman who goes around the city looking for a zipless fuck. It was basically an occasion for a photographer to take pictures—I mean good pictures, suitable for *National Geographic*—of half-dressed models pretending to have sex in different semipublic locations. There was no real reason for me to be there. I just liked the leggy photographer. She specialized in rockers, and she treated me as if I were Wayne Coyne, an aging, second-tier celebrity whose second-tierness was exactly what made him hip. We met in what was nominally a strip club. Under a recent city ordinance, however, it had become illegal for women to show their nipples in public, so all the venue could offer was some sad girls in bras jogging dully in place on a platform behind the bar, ignored by everybody. "Do you know what the chicks who work in these places call them?" the photographer asked me. It'd been years since I'd heard anyone use the word "chicks." "Stopless bars."

"Not tipless bars?"

She laughed in my ear. "That's good. I'm going to tell that to somebody."

We collected the female model, who was a friend of hers, and took taxis from one location to the next. At each stop, our protagonist would pose with a different partner, a waxy corporate mannequin, a bike messenger with a mane of tumbling black curls, a bouncy exotic dancer who kept snapping off backbends. The night got hotter and more humid until, as we were hauling our gear between locations, the sky burst with a biblical roar, and we were pummeled with what might have been lead shot. For the rest of the night, we did our work to the drumming of falling water. We went from the photographer's apartment building to a boutique hotel on the Upper East Side and back to her apartment. By then it was early morning, and we were all exhausted. The model could barely prop herself up on some pillows to fondle the exotic dancer. When the photographer told her she could get dressed, she let out a groan of relief and called her boyfriend to come pick her up. I stayed behind to help with the lights. Outside it was still raining. "You're never going to get a taxi," the photographer told me. We looked at each other. Her eyes were blue but looked black because of her makeup. I don't remember whether F. was down in the city that night. She may have been traveling. Regardless of where she was, she'd put no pressure on me to come home and would be unlikely to question me too closely even if I were to walk in while the neighborhood parents were seeing their kids off to preschool in the street below. This reticence is one of her most attractive features, and also one of her most unnerving. In somebody else, it might indicate a fear of learning something unpleasant, but I think F.'s reticence has more to do with her sense of dignity, her fear of debasing yours or sacrificing her own. In either case, I wouldn't have to lie.

Still, I left. I could say that I was thinking of the vows I was supposed to recite in another few months or that between the photographer and F. there was no choice. But, really, who was asking me to make a choice? (The allure of infidelity—one of the allures—is the allure of not choosing. You can have both.) It may be more correct to say that I had too vivid a picture of how I'd feel on waking up next to the photographer, how anxious I'd be to get away, and how anxious I'd be not to seem too eager about it, which would—I knew this from earlier occasions, before I met F.—make me stay later and later, until she'd either gotten the wrong impression or was good and sick of me. It may be that much of my loyalty to F. arises from my sense that she is the only person I wouldn't, to one extent or another, want to get away from when I woke beside her in the morning, not because she's the person I'm sanctioned to wake beside but because of all the people I might wake or have woken up beside, she is the only one with whom I can feel alone, as in the Frank O'Hara poem that ends, "You are emptying the world so we can be alone."

It may also be that I realized that the photographer wasn't sending me sexual signals so much as observing professional etiquette. Feature reporters have to pretend they're fascinated by everybody they interview, and maybe people who photograph rock stars have to keep up the impression that they're aroused by everybody on a shoot, even extending the courtesy to writers. I could say that being present on a sex shoot had an effect opposite to that of looking at the resulting photographs. It was too much process. When I think back to what I saw through the photographer's viewfinder, I recall the highlights on a man's pecs, the inky Möbius of a twisted bra strap, the fraught synapse between an upright nipple and a suppliant tongue. How many angels might waltz in that gap. When I think back to what I saw in front of me, though, I remember the photographer making her model friend sit up for a shot rather than lie back because if she lay back her tits would pancake to the side. The model was tired, and she complained, but I could see the photographer was right.

She was right about taxis too. The whole way home, one after another skidded past me, stuffed with grateful passengers or with its "Off Duty" sign burning like a brand. I had to walk blocks before I found an empty one, and by then I was so wet I might as well have saved myself the ten bucks.

In both cats and humans, it's mostly the male that roams in pursuit of sex. The rule, however, isn't ironclad. Many years ago I had a friend whom a teenaged diving accident had left a paraplegic. He couldn't get hard-ons. He once came to me upset because he'd learned that just before they got married, his wife had had sex with another man. She'd wanted to know if she could bear to go the rest of her life without fucking, and she knew of no way to be sure without actually doing it, as it turned out, with a neighbor in their apartment complex. She'd decided she could. Somebody else might have treated this as grounds for divorce. My friend stayed with his wife. A few years later, he was surgically outfitted with a penis pump that enabled him to have intercourse as often and as long as he wanted. He and his wife were happy for many years until he died from complications from his old injury.

"Do you want to know what I felt then?"

"I'm not sure I want to know."

"I felt desire."

~~~

At some point on the night of September 29, I went into my office and tried Skyping F. at the residency, which was how we'd been talking. The phone, or I guess the computer, rang in that strange, wet way, as if each ring were a bubble rising through hundreds of feet of green-black water from the hold of a ship sunken on the sea floor. In my mind, the horizontal distance between us translated into a vertical distance. I was the one at the bottom. No one answered. Well, where F. was, it was long after midnight. She'd probably shut down her laptop for the night.

Earlier in the day, she'd sent me an e-mail that ended with a question about the financial tidal wave that had begun sweeping the world a few weeks before, snatching up trillions of dollars in its rush. She wanted to know if we were going to lose our retirement savings. "Possibly yes," I wrote back now. "I'll tell you more yesterday. Bruno told me that Biscuit's been gone for 2 days, and I'm sick with worry. I'm waiting to hear more from him—Sherri's been helping him look for her—but I may fly up there this weekend to see if I have better luck." I was already thinking of going up to New York to look for Biscuit myself.

It's only on rereading this message that I realize I typed "yesterday" when I meant "tomorrow."

~~~

A while after we had Biscuit spayed, I became conscious of a high-pitched whine that seemed to be coming from just outside my office. I thought it might be somebody doing construction down the block or a disturbance in the phone lines. But I couldn't figure out what kind of power tool would make a sound like that, steadily, for hours on end, and when I called the phone company, I was assured that their lines had never been known to whine. F. came into the room, listened quizzically in that way she has, standing very still with her small, dear head cocked to one side, and then said she thought the sound was coming from inside the house. "You're crazy," I told her. Then I put my ear against the wall. I recoiled as if it were on fire. Up close, the sound was enveloping. It wasn't a whine; it was a drone, shrill enough to make the hair on my arms stand on end and at the same time inward, meditative, monastic.

The wall was infested with bees. F. worried about being stung, but I thought it more likely we'd be driven mad, or I would be; I was the one who worked in that room. Now that I knew what was making it, the hum, which before had been merely puzzling, gave me the creeps. I asked the landlord for advice on driving out an infestation of bees. "Drive them out? Jesus, you don't 'drive them out.'" He was large and red faced, and his politics were to the right of the emperor Nero's, but I respected his industry and lack of bullshit, and I think it amused him to see somebody who worked with his mind proposing to drive out vermin. He came over, drilled a hole in the Sheetrock, sprayed in some industrial-grade bug killer, then capped the hole with a butterfly screw. We waited for the humming to stop. It didn't. Outside the window I saw a dark plume of bees issue from the side of the house like smoke and hang in the air, but it was just a detachment from the main colony. We pulled out the screw and quickly jammed the bug spray can's

nozzle into the hole before bees could pour out of it and added
a few more lethal squirts. This time, the humming seemed to
get louder. It sounded angry. I told my wife, "We'd better not
go outside." Biscuit had jumped up on a chair and was staring
with interest at the screw in the wall. F. picked her up. "And
keep the cats in."

The killing took almost three days. When it became clear
that spraying inside the house was only displacing small numbers of insects, the landlord sent over some workmen to drill
holes in the outer wall, especially in the insulation around the
chimney. Then they tore off a soffit and sprayed there. Even
with the windows shut, the house stank. We worried about our
central nervous systems, and about the cats', which were more
sensitive. Every time Biscuit raced across the floor for no reason
or rolled onto her side and tried to disembowel a table leg with
her hind feet, we thought the worst. The humming mounted;
the bees stormed out in greater numbers, like cavalry making
sorties from a besieged fortress. The workmen sweltered beneath the July sun in padded jackets and canvas gloves. The
cats clamored to go out. At some point the extermination began
to take effect. Soon there were no bees by the back door. Then,
in a coordinated assault, the landlord drilled a second hole in
the office wall, and the two of us sprayed in more bug killer in
unison. Along with the cans of Bee Gone, he'd brought along a
sprayer, the kind with a pump that you see in old cartoons, with
no markings on it, but he didn't use that yet.

The buzzing surged, and for a moment it was as if we were
inside a huge electrical transformer. A curtain of insects blackened the air from above the window almost to the ground. The

landlord threw the window open and worked the pump of his archaic sprayer. The curtain fell. It fell all at once, as if cut loose from an invisible rod, with a soft patter. Afterward the yard was crunchy with tiny, desiccated corpses. I worried that Biscuit would eat them and be poisoned, but she steered clear of them. She may have been repelled by the stench of whatever it was that had come out of that unmarked canister or simply been uninterested in something that was already dead. Unlike dogs, cats have no taste for carrion.

I have stated my problem with the term "forbidden fruit"—I mean its association with the apple of the Tree of Knowledge, which probably wasn't an apple at all. Adam and Eve may have eaten that fruit in spite of God's injunction, but they didn't eat *because* of it. The true forbidden fruit may be the pears Augustine writes about in the *Confessions*. He was sixteen. They grew on a tree close to his family's vineyard in Thagaste, and neither their color nor their flavor was special:

> But late one night, having prolonged our games in the streets until then, as our bad habit was—a group of young scoundrels, and I among them, went to shake and rob this tree. We carried off a huge load of pears, not to eat ourselves, but to dump out to the hogs, after barely tasting some of them ourselves. Doing this pleased us all the more because it was forbidden.

Augustine, by the way, believed that before the Fall, sex was a purely voluntary act and not the tortured impulse it has been ever since. Adam willed his erections the way somebody wills a handshake. When he did, however, he was probably being more than just friendly.

The Animals in the Garden of Eden

This is a Gnostic legend from the early Christian era. Because God created Adam and Eve as vegetarians ("Behold, I have given you every plant yielding seed which is upon the face of all the earth, and every tree with seed in its fruit; you shall have them for food"), they really had no need of the animals over which they had been given dominion, not even the beasts of burden, for they could get all the food they wanted without plowing, and they had no possessions that had to be carried. Nor did the animals need people, and so in those first days they kept mostly to themselves. The only exceptions were the dog and the cat. The dog already liked humans—Adam, especially, who threw him sticks—and the cat was curious about them. They were so outlandish. Of all the creatures in the Garden, they alone had no fur and walked upright on their hind legs, and whenever they saw the cat, they made a sound that in time he understood was meant to make him come to them. Sometimes he did.

And so on the day Adam and Eve ate the fruit of the Tree of Knowledge, the dog and the cat were nearby. When Adam took a bite of the fruit Eve had given him, the dog came closer, wagging his tail and grinning as if to ask, "Maybe something for me?" And Adam tore off some of the fruit and gave it to him. It was the first time a human had fed an animal by hand or, indeed, fed one at all. Now the cat came up to them. He did it only out of curiosity, but the woman thought he was hungry, so she took a piece of the fruit, a small piece because it was so sweet and so nice and already she was inflamed by a feeling no one had ever felt before—greed—and held it out in her hand as the man had done with the dog. The cat approached and sniffed the fruit, his tail flicking, but he wouldn't eat it. No one thought to lay the fruit on the ground—where the cat still might not have eaten it—and in the next moment the woman gave in to her greed and ate the fruit herself, sucking the pulp from her fingers and sighing because she wished there were more. The cat watched her.

Then God came, and they knew what they had done. He sentenced the people to unceasing toil and the pangs of childbirth and, saving the worst for last, death. Then he looked at the dog and the cat. What was he going to do with them? The dog, sensing trouble, hung his head and began to whimper. The cat looked up at God. I don't know if it was the dog's crying or the cat's unblinking gaze that softened him. "Well, I only warned those two," God said to himself. "Those *people*." It was the first time that anyone had ever spoken in a voice filled with disgust. He looked at the animals. "How were these ones supposed to know? The poor, dumb creatures." And so they were spared everything except death. That was nonnegotiable.

But from then on, the Lord added, the animals' fate would be tied up with that of the humans, for if they hadn't taken part in the humans' sin, they had still been its witnesses. He asked them what they wanted to do. The dog said, "Let me go with the people, even out of Paradise, and wander with them over the earth. I'll help them get their food, and I'll sleep with them by their fires, and when the woman has babies, I'll stand guard over them, for they are weak creatures." And God said, "Good dog! Go with my blessing."

But the cat didn't want to go with the people. He liked them well enough, but it was the Garden he was attached to, its high, soft grasses, its encyclopedia of smells. "Let me stay in this place and be its familiar spirit until you see fit to let the man and the woman back in. When you do, I'll be there to welcome them." And God said, "Good cat! Abide here with my blessing."

This is why dogs stay close to people and travel at their side, following the example of their first ancestor. And this is why cats stay in the house, or nearby, in emulation of the one cat who dwells in Paradise, waiting for the people to return. On that day, he will greet the man and the woman at the gate and braid himself about their ankles, gazing up at them and purring. In the meantime, he keeps the mice down.

3

$\mathcal{E}$ARLY ON THE MORNING OF SEPTEMBER 30, UNABLE TO sleep, I began researching airfares to New York. I had classes till Thursday, so I couldn't leave before October 2, and of course flying on that short notice would cost more than I could afford. Really, anything would. Every month my salary from the university was instantly siphoned off by two rents and two sets of utility bills, along with payments to the banks I was into for some $60,000. When I wasn't teaching, I cowered inside the house, afraid the last bills would fly from my pockets the moment I stepped outside. But what was I supposed to do? I thought of our poor Gattino, who'd vanished from the yard the year before and had probably died alone, thousands of miles from where he'd been born. I thought of Biscuit wandering through the lank fall undergrowth, hungry and dazed. I thought of college kids racing down the back roads in fast cars bought for them by enabling parents. I thought of coyotes. I don't have any special powers where cats are concerned—

where anything is concerned. But at least Biscuit usually came when I called her. Maybe she'd come for Sherri; she liked Sherri, or she liked the food Sherri poured into her dish almost as dependably as F. and I did, and I'm sure more dependably than Bruno, who couldn't be trusted to return a phone call and, if you want to know the truth, seemed a little afraid of cats. And so I told myself that Biscuit would come when she heard Sherri's voice. That is, *if* she heard it. She might not be able to.

After going through a bunch of travel websites, I opted for the discount airline that flew out of Myrtle Beach, an hour and a half away. A round-trip flight to La Guardia would cost me $302.50 plus $63 in fees. It was still too much. I let the cursor hover over the "Buy Now" button; I may have clicked on it a couple times and then canceled. I cursed Bruno and F. and even Biscuit and then prayed that God or whatever not take those curses seriously—I was just joking. Finally, I sent Bruno an e-mail telling him I'd be coming up on October 2 to look for Biscuit unless he or Sherri found her first. He should let me know by the end of the day. I hoped it didn't read like an ultimatum, but of course that's what it was.

~ ~ ~

Here are some of the places I've seen her sleep:

On the frayed red modular sofa in the living room, beside the remote control I'd left there the night before. Stirring, she'd knock it to the floor, and the soft thump of its impact would wake her. She wouldn't be startled. She'd only open her eyes, turn her head to see what the noise was, maybe going so far as to roll onto her back and let her head loll over the edge of the seat cushion until she saw the control lying on the rug. Then, satisfied—and to me her satisfaction suggests at least a rudimentary sense of causality, an intimation that the sound that roused her was somehow connected to the object that once had once been *up here* and was now *down there*—she'd go back to sleep.

On the chair that used to be the sofa's center module but that we kept off to the side for guests.

On the wooden radiator cover.

Before the fireplace, on the polka-dot rug that we rolled up and took down to the basement after it got stained with massage oil.

In the wedge of sunlight that fell onto the kitchen counter between noon and four in the afternoon. I know you're not supposed to allow animals on surfaces where you prepare food, and if F. and I were running a restaurant, this would be enough to get us cited by the health department.

On the floor of F.'s bedroom closet, in the corner between a heating duct and a hanging shoe bag. This was the most se-cluded of her sleeping spots, the one where she was least likely to be disturbed by a human or another cat. In it, she was con-cealed almost completely. Several times when looking for her, I'd open the door, glance around, and decide she wasn't there until I saw her paw emerge from behind a hatbox like the hand of a sleeper groping for a ringing alarm clock. I suppose that's what I was to her, a clock she didn't set and didn't know how to turn off but wasn't especially bothered by since, unlike F. or me, she never had trouble going back to sleep—never.

In the back of the car, until the night I was driving to the station to pick up F. after she'd spent the day in the city and I felt something supple and alive graze my shoulder and nearly drove into the oncoming traffic before I swung the wheel the other way and nearly drove into a ditch instead. It was Biscuit, climbing onto the headrest. When I swerved, she dropped onto the front passenger seat and looked up at me, her ears tipped forward, her upturned muzzle soft and pale in the glow of the dash. The smartest thing would have been to turn around and deposit her back at the house, but I was already late. I drove on. During the next thirty minutes, she paced along the seatbacks, explored the junk in the cargo area, and, briefly, investigated the gas and brake pedals before I kicked her away—lightly, with no more violence than I'd kick her away from the front door if I were coming in with some heavy bags of groceries, just more urgency. At some point she returned to the seat beside me and stayed there for the rest of the drive. She was calm, except for a two- or three-mile stretch when she meowed repeatedly, maybe overwhelmed by the speed with which trees and cars and houses swept past in the dark or by the lights that shot at us from the northbound lanes, guttering in the rain. I've read that cats can't process visual information that comes at them too quickly. She quieted when I stroked her. On reaching the station, I pulled her into my lap, afraid she might otherwise bound out when I opened the door for my wife. She wasn't crazy about that. Still, she was pleased to see F. and was well behaved for most of the drive back. From then on, I always made sure to roll up the windows when I parked in the driveway.

On my bed. When she was first living with us, Biscuit used to curl up on the pillow next to mine about an hour before I retired. It didn't matter if that was at midnight or two in the morning; she might have been monitoring my melatonin levels. She never took my pillow, but she seemed to think of the other one as hers and, on nights F. slept with me, was disgruntled at having to give up her spot. Sometimes she swiped at F. when she shooed her off, for although she was a mostly good-natured cat, she could be testy. A few years ago, she started sleeping on my stomach or between my legs. I guess she liked the warmth, and being contained in the stockade of her owner's limbs may have made her feel more secure. I obliged her by sleeping on my back and was careful not to disturb her if I had to get up to piss. It took some minor acrobatics, but I was grateful that she chose to be so close to me.

Did she choose? I think of choice as the trait that cats, maybe more than any other species, share with human beings. At least they seem to choose, often with every appearance of thought, though "thought" is probably the wrong word and will invite scorn from animal behaviorists. They circle a room with a connoisseurial air, considering the best place to sit. One of those places may be beside their owner, but it may not be. It depends. Before an open door, they waver, weighing the options of coming in or staying outside. "Jesus Christ!" you yell, especially in winter, when with every second of their indecision you visualize dollars roaring up the chimney. If you were yelling at a dog, it would slink in on the instant, its whole being weighed down by shame. Your cat is unmoved. It looks at you; its tail lashes. This may be a sign that the animal is of two minds or just annoyed. You say, "All right," and close the door. A moment later there's a scrape of claws. Your cat has *chosen* to come in.

The sleeping places listed above are located in different houses F. and I have lived in during our time together. The fireplace was in our old house on Parsonage Street, the first house we shared as a couple; it was one of the reasons we rented it, along with the pattern of blue and white diamonds painted on the living room floor. We had the sofa when we lived there; it was F.'s and predated me by eight or nine years. But when I picture Biscuit sleeping on it, it's in the living room of the house on Avondale Road, with its sinking toilet and rippling floors that were too thin to be sanded; I had to settle for waxing them, and F. thought I was insane even to do that, since it wasn't our house and she was pissed at the landlord. The basement was in the house on Parsonage Street, the one on Avondale Road being too small and filthy to store anything in, and prone to flooding besides. The Parsonage Street basement was dirty enough. It's where we took Biscuit when she came back with paint on her muzzle, on the theory that there was nothing down there she could fuck up. We were wrong.

I don't know why Biscuit slept with me rather than with F. We were introduced to her at the same time. But it was me she came up to first and my hand she began licking. In the same way, Zuni made a beeline for F. when we came to look at her at her breeder's, who was giving her away because her kittens weren't show quality. She was already full-grown, plush and tubby, a little matronly. We tried to play with her by rolling a ball back and forth between us, and the tabby followed it, but on seeing me she started in horror and scrambled underneath a cabinet. Maybe her early experience had imprinted her with a fear of men. The breeder's husband hunted and practiced taxidermy, and the house was filled with the stuffed corpses of his victims, which stared down from the walls, rigid with shock and indignation. Even now, seven years after we got her, Zuni barely lets me pet her. She only sleeps with F., and if I happen to be sharing the bed that night, she marches over me on her way to my wife with about as much consideration as the Wehrmacht gave valiant little Holland as it rolled across Europe to the sea.

I'm not sure this preference is the same thing as love. Did Biscuit love the red sofa? Did she love the kitchen counter? Did she love the rise and fall of my stomach as she lay on it in the dark, waiting to be lulled to sleep? Does Zuni love F.? Did Bitey love the little boy, a refugee from a treeless city neighborhood where the nightly chimes of the ice cream truck were sometimes interrupted by gunfire, who spent three days with us one summer back when she was still alive, only to be carried away in tears?

Wilfredo thought she loved him because she slept on his bed and not Cedric's. Originally, F. and I were just going to have Cedric, but as we were getting ready to meet his bus, we got a call from a counselor who wanted to know if we could take in a second kid whose Friendlytown Family had backed out at the last minute. My wife stared at the phone; if it had had a cord, she would have been twisting it around her wrist. It had been her idea to have an eight-year-old from the city stay with us for two weeks, but now she was anxious. What would we feed Cedric? What if he got homesick? What if he hated us? How would we keep him entertained? I told her that taking the other kid would solve the last problem. "Kids don't want to be with grown-ups," I told her. With each passing minute, the enterprise was feeling more and more like an enterprise, or, as some of my relatives would have said, a *production*, something that required a script and stage managers and might still get lousy reviews. Still, there was no way out of it. It was *our* production, this thing we were doing together. "They want to be with other kids."

When I look back, what astonishes me is not that I was so naive but that I was so forgetful of my own childhood, whose most traumatic episodes occurred when I was placed in a cage with other kids and told to have fun. Cedric was small and quick and lithe. Wilfredo was big and soft and slow moving, with a round, shaved head. There was something muffled about him, as if he'd been wrapped in dense cotton batting in order to protect him, but at the cost of an entranced, blinking passivity. What nobody had told us, least of all the charity that sent him to us, was that he was only six. When I put him on a bike, Wilfredo wobbled and capsized. It was just a child's bike, purple with chopper handlebars, and I caught him before he hit the ground, but still he cried and Cedric taunted him. Taunting was Cedric's operative mode. He taunted Wilfredo even after he'd learned to stay upright and more or less keep pace with us as we wheeled in and out of the shade of the maples on the neighborhood's mercifully empty streets.

"Man, what's wrong with you? You can't go no faster? You slowing us down."

"I can go fast," Wilfredo muttered. "You just go too fast."

Right after that, he bumped Cedric's rear wheel, or maybe Cedric bumped him. But it was Wilfredo who went down, and this time I wasn't able to catch him. He skinned his knee. "He tripped me," he cried, his voice thick with outrage. Cedric accused Wilfredo of trying to trip *him.*

"Come on, nobody tried to trip anybody," I said. "It was an accident. Wilfredo's just learning." But of course, in saying this, I was implying that the accident was Wilfredo's fault. And I was showing my bias. Already, I preferred the mean, quick kid to the slow, gentle one. You could tell he was gentle even when he told Cedric he was going to fuck him up.

That was later, after dinner and a game of catch played with sofa cushions on the front lawn in the dusk while lightning bugs winked around us like tiny flashbulbs, and a bath that started out well—the boys wanted to take one together, which made us think they were finally starting to get along—but ended with Cedric bursting out of the bathroom, shaking off water and yelling that Wilfredo had peed in the tub. Wilfredo said he hadn't peed. He'd followed Cedric into their bedroom. Unlike the older boy, he didn't mind being wet. He stood with his towel drooping below his dimpled belly and a puddle of water gathering on the floor between his feet. His denial wasn't convincing; it held a note of secret pride.

"Listen," I told him. "You don't pee in the tub, that's just gross."

"But I didn't pee, man!"

"I'm not saying you did pee. But you don't do it." I saw the illogic of this. "You cannot pee in the tub."

"You pee, Wilfredo," Cedric insisted. His disgust, if it had been real to begin with, had given way to triumph. "I saw you pee, man. You nasty! You a nasty, ugly bighead."

That was when Wilfredo threatened to fuck him up.

"Hey!" I barked. Where had I learned to bark like that? Wilfredo was taller than Cedric and probably outweighed him by thirty pounds, but there was no way of predicting how a fight between them might end. As I later learned, when I had to wrestle Cedric off the golf cart of a security guy who'd brought us home from the county fair after the kid had a tantrum outside the tent where the Jack Russell agility trials were supposed to happen, he had a grasping, clawing, elastic strength that was wholly out of proportion to his size.

For most of the day, the cats had avoided the boys, but now Bitey entered the room. She brushed against me and then approached the children, staying just out of reach. Most cats approach kids this way, and it's easy to mistake it for teasing until you reflect that even a small child is ten times the size of a cat. Bitey didn't look fearful. Her tail was up, and her underslung jaw gave her the air of something looking for a fight, or at least not shying away from one. "Don't grab her," F. warned. "Just put out your hand like this." She demonstrated, holding hers at cat's eye level, then scratching the upraised chin. "Hello, Bitus, you noble creature. Let her come to you."

I don't remember if either boy was able to pet her. Bitey could be affectionate, but on her own terms. A year before, she'd disappeared for a month before showing up at a house on the other side of town. During that time, I did little but look for her, putting up flyers, riding my bike for miles in every direction while imploringly shouting her name to the winds, stopping every so often to rattle the container of dry food I kept in my knapsack. But when I came to be reunited with her at her rescuers', my heart so swollen with love I might only have been its caddy, the flunky whose job it was to carry a heart around while it throbbed and felt, she barely gave me a glance and sauntered past me to inspect a flower in the yard. When I picked her up, she struggled. Maybe she'd forgotten whose cat she was, or maybe I was being reminded of the futility of the phrase "whose cat." The woman who'd found her had grown attached to her, and I invited her to come by our house the next day. Stoically, I'd decided that if Bitey wasn't happy with F. and me, maybe she'd be better off with her. I think the woman had the same idea. She showed up looking hopeful. But now, Bitey ignored her while coiling and coiling around my ankles, grinning so widely you could see the pale pink washboard of her palate and purring cynically.

I left the room while F. read to the boys from a book about a farting dog. When I came back, Bitey was lying at the foot of Wilfredo's bed; it was really a folding cot we'd borrowed from someone. She lay facing away from him with her paws straight out before her, like a little sphinx, her eyes slitted. "What's that cat's name?" Wilfredo asked. F. told him, and he announced, "Bitey loves me." His mother hadn't packed pajamas for him (later we'd learn he didn't own any); he was wearing underpants and some team's T-shirt. I don't think we knew yet that he was only six, but still it struck me that he was just a little boy who might be away from home for the first time in his life. The night yawning around the house was so much darker than the night he was used to, and alive with digestive chirps and gulps and stridulations. But the cat had come to him. F. told him it was because Bitey was a good judge of character. I beamed at her. We'd done good.

Of course, this was usually my bedroom, so Bitey was used to sleeping in it, and if she lay down on Wilfredo's cot instead of on the bed with Cedric, it may have been because she was drawn to the younger boy's particular smell of hot dogs, ketchup, bug spray, and bath soap, with a faint, interesting undernote of piss.

Back when I was teaching comp in grad school and despairing over the blandness of the suggested essay topics, I hit on having students write about their last girlfriend or boyfriend. They had to begin by telling how they'd met, what had attracted them to the other person, and the kinds of things they'd enjoyed doing together (I didn't tell them that they couldn't write about sex, but nobody ever did). In the concluding paragraphs, they had to draw on those examples to define what makes a good girlfriend or boyfriend. I still remember some of the kids' responses:

> To me, a good boyfriend is somebody who cares.
> Someone who thinks I'm special.
> She makes me feel like I'm important.
> I can have a good time with him.

No one in my recollection said anything about love. This may be due to the same reticence that kept the kids from writing about sex (unless that's what the last author meant by "a good time"). Maybe they thought it was creepy of me to even be asking them about their girlfriends and boyfriends. But maybe they already knew that love has about as much to do with what makes someone a good girlfriend or boyfriend as it does with what makes someone a good wife or husband, which is not a whole lot. More, in the second case, but even there the relation is not so much necessary as contingent.

Love is a feeling, and girlfriend or boyfriend, like wife or husband, is a function, or maybe a job; you could think of a date as a job interview. My students were trying to define the qualifications for that job the way personnel directors might mull over the requisite skill set of a CEO or a die-punch operator. You could argue with some parts of this analogy: employees, for one thing, usually get paid. But you choose the people you go out with the same way you choose the ones who work for you, down to the guy with a van you hire for a couple hours to move a bookcase. That's why you find notices for both on Craig's List:

I'm hoping to find a man who is also educated, intelligent, healthy, a non-smoker, employed, enjoys travel, culture and trying new things and who too wants companionship, friendship and hopefully ultimately a LTR. I go to the gym 4 to 5 times a week and hope you are also fit and take care of yourself. If you are looking for a FWB, hook up, fling, or NSA relationship than I am definitely not the woman for you. So if you think you might be what I'm looking for, please say hello and tell me about yourself.

We all want the same thing. That person that will care for us, listen, comfort us, make us feel special, never hurt us, accept us for who we are, and basically love us unconditionally until the end of time. We want a friend, a lover, a companion because no one wants to grow old alone. We need that person who will nudge us when we're sleeping and stop breathing so we don't wake up dead (lol).

So, I've found a great house to buy. Now I just need a man to share it with. Man must:
1. Have a retirement plan.
2. Believe in aliens.
3. Be comfortable in most any social situation.

What's striking about these ads is the way they combine specificity and generality, skepticism and idealism: only somebody very idealistic expects to find unconditional love in adulthood. Their specificity is the specificity of the educated consumer who knows what she wants or, more commonly, what she doesn't want (e.g., a smoker, an FWB, or an NSA relationship). Even so, consumers may sometimes be overwhelmed by the abundance of choices available to them, and the variety, the latter suggested by such categories as Strictly Platonic, Men Seeking Women, Women Seeking Men, Men Seeking Men, Women Seeking Women, Casual Encounters, and Misc. Romance. This vertigo, the vertigo of the shopper staring dazedly into the ice cream freezer at the supermarket, may be the source of the posters' vagueness. And, of course, much of the language they use has no agreed-on definition. Is a "casual encounter" the same thing as a one-night stand, and if not, how many encounters can you have before they stop being casual? Does "LTR" mean a lifetime relationship or just a long-term one, and how long is long-term? And is "lifetime relationship" an anachronism, as meaningless as the wish for someone who will love us to the end of time?

There were no personal ads in the Middle Ages. To the extent that people chose at all, they chose spouses from a narrow pool of neighbors or, more likely, had spouses chosen for them by their fathers or male guardians. (Doubtless, there were also casual encounters and misc. romances back then; that's why we have the fabliaux.) It was the difference between shopping at the Whole Foods and at the local farmers' market, your dad standing beside you at the produce stand, reaching over you to squeeze the plums. "He'll take these." What did those people want, our great-great-many-times-great grandparents, with their bad hygiene and their lives brief as a struck match? In the case of the upper classes, we know what their fathers wanted. It was they who drew up the marriage contracts:

I, Thibaut, count palatine of Champagne and Brie, make known to all, present and future, that my loyal and faithful Guy of Bayel and his wife Clementia have made a marriage contract in my presence with Jocelin of Lignol for the marriage of their son Herbert with Jocelin's daughter Emeline. These are the clauses:

[1] Guy has given to his son whatever he had at Bayel, at the village called Les Mez, and at Bar-sur-Aube and within those village districts, including tenants, woods, lands, and all other things.

[2] Jocelin has given his daughter Emeline an annual rent of 5*l*. [from his property] that will be assigned by two other men, one to be named by Guy and the other by Jocelin. And Jocelin will give his daughter 100*l*. cash [as dowry], which is to be invested in income-producing property by the two appointed men within one year after the marriage.

[3] Peter Guin [of Bar-sur-Aube, chamberlain of Champagne and Jocelin's father-in-law] and his son Guy affirmed in my presence that they gave whatever they had at Les Mez to Emeline or to Jocelin's other daughter Lucy, whom Herbert earlier had engaged to marry.

[4] Herbert will hold the above mentioned 5*l*. rent, the property purchased with the 100*l*. cash, as well as the land at Les Mez, in fief and liege homage from Guy, son of my faithful chamberlain Peter Guin, save liegeance to me and save the liegeance contracted to anyone else before the marriage.

[5] Guy of Bayel and Clementia agreed that if Emeline dies before the marriage, they will have Herbert marry another of Jocelin's daughters when she becomes nubile, under the same terms.

Beyond the exchange of property, there was some doubt as to what a marriage was or how it was delimited, especially in the early Middle Ages, when the church hadn't yet elevated it to a sacrament. As late as the fifteenth century, a lawsuit arose in Troyes over whether a young couple could have their union performed by one of their friends, in the street, or whether they needed a public figure, a schoolmaster, to do it, or a real priest, or whether they could just as legitimately take the vows on their own, without anybody officiating. The vows might be short; for example: "I swear to thee, Marguerite, that I will love no other woman but thee to the day of my death." "Paul, I pledge my word that I will have no other husband than you to the day of my death." (In the French, Paul addresses his fiancée in the familiar second person, *tu*; Marguerite uses the formal *vous*.) Symbolic gifts would be exchanged. The couple would shake hands or kiss. Sometimes, the boy would seal his commitment by putting his tongue in his beloved's mouth, announcing that he was doing it "in the name of marriage."

The last gesture suggests a popular attempt to resolve an old theological debate as to whether marriage was defined by a sexual act or a verbal one: by fucking or an oath. The first definition justified abducting and raping the young woman who caught your fancy, which explains those peasant ceremonies in which the groom and his friends pretended to kidnap the bride, who pretended to be upset about it. But it seemed like something was missing. In the twelfth century, Gratian formulated a two-part definition of marriage:

> It must be understood that betrothal begins a marriage, sexual union completes it. Therefore between a betrothed man and a betrothed woman there is marriage, but begun; between those who have had intercourse, marriage is established.

Other churchmen argued that all that was needed was the verbal consent of both parties, two people saying, "I do." After all, if sex was what made a marriage, one could say that Mary and Joseph had lived in sin.

It's startling to see how matter-of-fact the medieval church could be about sex, down to earnest discussions of the morality of the female orgasm and whether a woman whose husband came before she did was allowed to fondle herself: fourteen out of seventeen theologians said she could. It was a practical application of Paul's teaching: "The husband must give the wife what is due to her, and the wife equally must give her husband his due" (1 Cor. 7, 1–3). The idea of the debt, or *debitum*, informed all of marriage, gave shape to it the way the skeleton gives shape to the human body. It was the simple counterpart to elaborate contracts like the one between Guy and Jocelin, made not between two fathers but between a wife and a husband and governing not the division of property but the sharing of duty and pleasure. The poor had no property, but they could have orgasms, and people took it for granted that wives as well as husbands were entitled to them. *Just give me my propers when you get home.* Both Otis Redding and Aretha Franklin sing "R-E-S-P-E-C-T," and both their versions are considered definitive.

It makes sense that the church would concern itself with the pleasure of the married couple. A marriage in which both spouses get their propers will be fecund and stable, producing children for the glory of God and the increase of Mother Church. Satisfied spouses are less likely to go splashing around in the concupiscent puddles of the flesh. The sex the church sanctioned wasn't concupiscent. It was temperate, cheerful, orderly, the payment of a debitum. Who gets hot and bothered writing out the month's checks? Marriage was chiefly an economic relationship. Its purpose was to increase the property of propertied families or to maximize the labor of two individuals—and more, when children came—by joining them in a common domestic enterprise. In medieval art, the common people are often depicted laboring, the men in the fields, the women in the house. There's a painting I like in which three housewives stand proudly amid dozens of perfect cannonballs of dough they've rolled and patted into shape and are now feeding into a brick oven on an immense paddle. In their spotless dresses, they look as improbably put-together as June Cleaver vacuuming in her heels. Sometimes they work together, as in the images that show men and women picking cabbages (the man carries his in a basket balanced on his head) or harvesting olives.

The work wasn't easy. Think of the strength and endurance it took to cut wheat with a sickle and bind it into sheaves and heap up the sheaves in stooks, all day long, day after day in harvest time, beneath a sun that filled the entire sky. Think of the labor of shaking the olives from every tree in the grove, the leaves hissing and flashing silver, the tedium of gathering the fallen fruit and pressing it into oil. "Cursed is the ground because of you," God tells the first, fallen couple. "In toil shall you eat of it all the days of your life." These are the words that make Masaccio's Adam cover his face and weep. Yet in most of the medieval images, the men and women look happy or, if not happy, content. This may be testimony to the value of the debitum, not just the sexual debitum but the entire system of mutual credit and debit, boon and obligation, that formed the economy of marriage. Beyond its harsh beginnings, the haggling and ritual rape (and sometimes real rape, too, which the victim was expected to forget once the rapist did right by her), the system was pretty fair. And there was probably added comfort in the simple fact that wife and husband worked together—sometimes side by side—and not alone.

~~~

Inwardly, I'd vowed not to write Bruno another e-mail or leave another message on his voice mail until I heard from him, but I broke my promise later on September 30, when I sent him a "missing cat" flyer I'd made up when I was supposed to be reading students' manuscripts. I asked him to make copies of it and put them up around the college and, as long as he was up and about, on some phone poles, too, just the ones in the neighborhood.

I don't remember whether I consulted F. about the wording. She probably would have thought it was too much to mention Biscuit's sinus problem, and, really, I question why I did, since the photo would be enough to show anyone what she looked like. I may have wanted to explain the discharge under her eyes. I have few pictures of her that don't show some; it's embarrassing.

I left the reward unspecified because $100 seemed too cheap, and I didn't want to say $1,000 for fear it might incite scam artists or even a backwoods home invader. And anyway, I didn't have $1,000, though I guess I could have borrowed it.

~~~

REWARD

LOST CAT
Yellow/Orange Tabby

Our cat Biscuit disappeared from our house on the corner of Avondale and Cannon Roads on the evening of September 27th or 28th. She's a small yellow-orange tabby with short legs. She sniffs a lot because of a sinus problem. She's extremely friendly and will probably come to you if you call her name.

IF YOU FIND HER, OR EVEN SEE HER,
PLEASE CALL
[PHONE NUMBERS REDACTED]

The word "economy" comes from the Greek words *oikos*, "house," and *nomos*, "manager": hence, a household manager or steward. Traditionally, this was a man's job. The stewards in Jesus's parables are men, as is the Reeve, or steward, in *The Canterbury Tales*. Economics is a stereotypically male profession; witness the gender balance on the president's Council of Economic Advisors. Only at the turn of the twentieth century did home economics emerge as a field of study for young women. By the time F. and I were teenagers, it was a required subject in most public high schools, though only for girls. A few years later, in the purifying glare of the women's movement, it would vanish from many curricula. Maybe it would have been better if boys had had to take it too. Who isn't better off for knowing how to sew on a button? I don't know if home ec traditionally included learning how to pay bills. In many households, that was the wife's job, even if she did it with her husband's paycheck. F. and I have never worked out this aspect of our domestic economy. Both of us pay bills, grabbing the checkbook off each other's desks. Only I bother balancing the account. F. just writes down what she spent and waits for me to do the math.

The first time I thought that we might make a couple, I was living in a loft in a neighborhood that still went by the name of the industry that had vanished from it years before. The city's full of neighborhoods like that. With its high ceilings and ponderous, steel-sashed windows, the loft was a relic of that industrial past. The enormous radiator bolted to one wall was usually too hot to touch, but periodically it stopped working, and in no time the room would be cold, cold enough to make your breath steam.

After coming up several times in response to my heat com-
plaints, the super took me aside and explained that the radiator
needed to be bled from time to time and gave me a little, short-
stemmed key so I could do it myself. He winked. "Just don't tell
anybody where you got it from."

The trick was to turn the valve just until water started trick-
ling out and then shut it quickly. I did it so often I got good at
it, and when the radiator went out one December morning
while F. was staying with me, I was almost happy for the opportunity to do my impression of a mechanically competent person for her; we were so still so new to each other that she might
believe that person was the real me. I addressed the radiator,
fitted the tip of the valve into a matching slot in the key, and
gave it a turn. Then I gave it another. Then I cried out as the
valve shot into the air, narrowly missing my eye, and was followed by a jet of scalding water. I'm not sure "jet" is the right
word. "Jet" connotes something of limited duration; this water
kept coming and coming. Hotly, it gushed from the top of the
radiator and arced several feet before splashing back down. It
was like something in a national park that people stand around
and take pictures of. I groped on the floor for the valve, but it
had rolled out of sight, or else the water was already too deep
for me to see it. There was a particular horror in seeing how
quickly it spewed out, like blood from a wound. I cursed helplessly, monotonously. Sometimes I just moaned, "Oh no!" and
was seized with shame at what F. would think if she heard me,
a grown man, moaning over a leaking radiator.

She brought me a kitchen mitt. I could have kissed the
hand that gave me that mitt. It wasn't enough to plug the flow,

but with the mitt on I could slow it a little, and at least I wouldn't get scalded any more. Of course, I had to stand there with my mittened thumb jammed into the spraying radiator, like the intrepid Dutch boy at the dyke, while the water mounted around my ankles. F. thought I ought to call the super. I didn't want to. Have I mentioned that I was in the loft illegally? Not long afterward, the super called me. F. held the phone up to my ear so I could hear his small, angry voice berating me. Trying very hard to sound calm, I reminded him that I'd only been doing what he told me to, and he stopped. Maybe he was scared I'd tell management about the key. Shortly, he came up with three porters and capped the spill with a replacement valve while his assistants baled out tepid water gritty with iron clinkers that rattled in their buckets.

When they left, the floors were wet, and the books on the lowest shelves of the bookcase were sodden; I had to throw a lot of them away. I was starting to shiver. The radiator was pushing out heat again, but the loft had been cold for a while, and my pajamas were soaked. F., though still in her pajamas, an oversized men's pair in robin's egg blue flannel, was dry, partly because she'd stayed away from the radiator and partly because at some point she'd put on a pair of rain boots. They were bright red and came almost to her knees. Back then, she was dying her hair red, a sort of candy-apple red, and I remember noting, as I watched her gamely mopping the floor, that she was color coordinated: red hair, red boots, and blue pj's. The pj's went with her eyes. How diligent she looked to me. Her diligence had nothing heavy about it, as diligence so often does, the heaviness of the five-hundred-pound barbells of virtue and of the strongman deadlifting them with popping eyes. F.'s diligence was light and playful. She made mopping look like a game. Bitey seemed to think it was. She followed F. closely, darting as close to the mop head as she dared, then darting back, after throwing a punch or two at its dank tentacles. I doubt I consciously thought that being with F. would make domestic labor fun. Nothing makes it fun, except maybe amphetamines, and then only for some people. I had only an idea of lightness, lightness in the face of calamity, and I knew it had to do with her.

"You didn't hear me back there?" I asked.

"Of course I heard you. You kept going, 'Oh no!'" she said. Actually, what she said was, "Ooooh nooooo!" The despairing howl of a cartoon character falling down an elevator shaft. When she laughed, her nose wrinkled charmingly. Did she kiss me to take the sting out of it, or am I making that up? Maybe she hugged me. "Ooooh nooooo!"

The thing is, I recognized myself. That's what I sound like. That's what I feel like. Ooooh nooooo. Often.

An early description of the domestic cat is this one by one Bartholomew de Glanville, written in 1240:

A beast of uncertain hair and color. For some cat is white, some red, and some black, some calico and speckled in the feet and in the ears. . . . And hath a great mouth and saw teeth and sharp and long tongue and pliant, thin, and subtle. And lappeth therewith when he drinketh. . . . And he is a full lecherous in youth, swift, pliant and merry, and

leapeth and rusheth on everything that is before him and
is led by a straw, and playeth therewith; and is a right
heavy beast in age and full sleepy, and lieth slyly in wait
for mice and is aware where they be more by smell than
by sight, and hunteth and rusheth on them in privy
places. And when he taketh a mouse, he playeth therewith, and eateth him after the play. In time of love is hard
fighting for wives, and one scratcheth and rendeth the
other grieviously with biting and with claws. And he
maketh a ruthful noise and ghastful, when one proffereth
to fight with one another, and unneth is hurt when he is
thrown from a high place.

This was before cats were widely kept as pets. If they were
valued at all, it was chiefly as mousers. And, also, as Bartholomew
notes, for their pelts:

And when he hath a fair skin, he is as it were proud
thereof, and goeth fast about. And when his skin is burnt,
then he bideth at home. And is oft for his fair skin taken of
the skinner, and slain and flayed.

One should remember that the Middle Ages were a terrible
time for cats. At carnival, they were tortured for the amusement of the crowd, which may be the origin of the German
katzenmusik, a carnival procession. What could that music be
but howls? And in France, the feast of St. John the Baptist,
June 24, was celebrated by stuffing cats into a sack and tossing
it onto a bonfire. Two figures of speech of that period are "as

patient as a cat whose claws are being pulled out" and "as patient as a cat whose paws are being grilled."

You can't speak of the relationship between cats and humans as you can of the one between humans and dogs: as a partnership. No painting or tapestry shows cats joining in the hunt. They can't be trained to draw carts or sleds, or to herd sheep, or to sniff suitcases for contraband. A paradox of their domestication is that once they're fed regularly, they lose much of their aptitude for pest control, or at least their enthusiasm. One morning, in the same loft I've written of, I was awakened by soft thumps and sat up to see Bitey and Ching, who then was only middle-aged and fat rather than old and gaunt, sitting a few feet away from each other and staring at something on the floor. It was a mouse, which they were batting back and forth between them. They did it economically, moving only their forepaws. Flick. Pause. Flick. Pause. Flick, flick. Pause. The tempo was the tempo of badminton rather than that of squash. I got up, meaning to put a stop to the cruelty, and the cats abandoned their prey and raced downstairs to be fed. They may not have recognized a mouse as something that could be eaten. I figured it would vanish down a crack somewhere while I fed them. However, a few minutes later, it appeared in the kitchen. The cats were sluggish from their meal; it might easily have gotten past them. This was what it started to do, moving with frictionless speed across the floor. But then, suddenly, suicidally, the rodent changed course and rushed *toward* the gray tom. Maybe it was so overwhelmed by fear that its brain was seized by a kind of dyslexia that made it scramble safety and danger. The same thing has happened to me. Seeing the mouse bearing down on him, Ching did something even more inexplicable: he flopped onto one side. There was something languishing about the way he did it. The mouse, which really must have had something wrong with it, started burrowing under the vast, soft stomach like a child trying to sneak under a circus big top. Ching looked up at me and mewed. "Oh, for crying out loud," I said and picked up the rodent by the tail before it could smother down there. Then I took it out into the hallway to become somebody else's vermin.

Biscuit was a much better hunter. No sooner did we start letting her out than she began leaving corpses by the door, mice, mostly, but also moles and the occasional chipmunk, laid out on their backs with their sad, brown incisors bared to the sky. Sometimes, through speed or stealth, she'd succeed in bringing prey inside the house. On those occasions, she gave out a characteristic cry, half meow and half moan. I suppose it was a victory cry, but to me it always sounded distressed, and it was a while before I stopped taking it as a sign she'd been hurt and anxiously opening the door for her. Maybe she was just meowing with her mouth full. I once had to spend most of a day trying to rescue a chipmunk she'd sneaked inside, after I'd gotten her to drop it by loudly clapping my hands at her. I kept flushing the poor creature from different hiding places—between the springs on the underside of the chaise longue, behind a radiator, even inside the head of the vacuum cleaner—but the moment it surfaced, Biscuit would try to pounce on it, I'd have to shoo her away, and when I turned again, the chipmunk would have skittered to a new hiding place. If Biscuit had been a dog, she might have helped me find it—by pointing, for instance. But she wasn't a dog; she was a cat, and she wanted the chipmunk for herself, to eat or kill or just torture until she got tired of it—in any event, for her own pleasure. True, she might have left the dead chipmunk for me as an offering to a social superior, according to some theories, or because, as Paul Leyhausen puts it, I was filling the role of a "deputy kitten." Still, I would be only the incidental beneficiary of her bloodlust, like the unobjectionable charity—the Red Cross, the United Way—that the bank uses as a catchment basin for the spillover of its extortionate profits, maybe to make those profits seem a fraction less extortionate or to make its customers feel fractionally better about being extorted from. She wouldn't—and I know how petty this sounds—she wouldn't have killed the chipmunk *for me*.

Well, maybe it isn't petty. Most definitions of love, following Aristotle, incorporate the notion that its objects are ends in themselves rather than means to other ends. You can't love somebody because she's great in bed or looks terrific in an Alexander McQueen or makes a perfect ragú Bolognese. Or, rather, you can, but what you feel then isn't love. The preposition "because" indicates that the object is only an intermediate point in your pursuit of sex or beauty or good food, and as soon as her enthusiasm starts to flag or her arms get too hammocky for a strapless, you'll start charting out a different route. But the true beloved always occupies a terminal position. She's the last point on the map. A corollary is that in love, the beloved is the reason for doing something rather than that action's afterword or appendix. And so I imagine a state of affairs in which Biscuit had no interest in chipmunks, was utterly indifferent to them, but on seeing one, had the thought, This is something he will like or use, and acted accordingly. That would be love.

~~~

Bruno may have gotten the flyer, but I doubt he ever got around to posting it. At least, I never saw it when I came home, not on any of the phone poles along Avondale Road or on the doors or bulletin boards of the college buildings, not even of the dorm right behind our house that the kid could have walked to in his pajamas. And it's not as if someone would have bothered taking down a flyer for a lost pet. Nobody ever takes anything off those bulletin boards, except maybe when the kids go home for the summer. Months after we lost him, I was still coming across the signs we'd put up for our Italian cat. Every time I saw one, my heart would stop for a moment. Then, as always, it went back to beating.

~~~

I'm sorry to admit I didn't really like Wilfredo—the belly, the threats, the crying, the peeing. F. liked him—judging by the softness with which she looked at him that first night, she may already have loved him—but she felt she couldn't protect him from Cedric, and Cedric was the kid we'd made a commitment to; we'd promised his mother we'd take care of him. He kept calling Wilfredo "fat" and "bighead," and Wilfredo kept threatening to fuck him up, and we had to keep taking them off separately and watching them like hawks at mealtimes, and it got tiring. And so on the third day after his arrival, a Friendlytown Lady came over, tall, slouching, with the indolent sexual sneer of a Bianca Jagger, and, in the tone of someone announcing an unexpected—really, an unmerited—treat, told Wilfredo he was going away to stay with another family that had a swimming pool. But Wilfredo didn't want a swimming pool. He wanted to stay with F. and me in the house of the four cats. That's what he kept calling it. "I want to stay in the house of the four cats!" The cry might have been translated from another language; its foreignness made it more plaintive. By then, the Friendlytown Lady had stopped pretending to be jolly. I'd like to make her the villain of this story, and it's true she was insensitive and officious. She might never have met a child in her life. But it was F. and I who'd decided Wilfredo had to leave, and I was the one who pried him off the banister that he clutched with both hands like a sailor holding onto a mast in a gale, his body stretched almost horizontal, wailing at the top of his lungs. F. was crying, too, silently. It was only the second or third time I'd seen her cry. At one point, even the Friendlytown Lady looked like she might cry. Only Cedric seemed pleased. "Ha ha, you go away!" he sang in Wilfredo's ear. His delicate features writhed with malice. But then he blocked the stairs with his outspread arms to keep me from carrying the other boy away. I pushed past him, holding Wilfredo against my chest. He sobbed and thrashed, he was as heavy as sack concrete, as heavy as the weights they lash to the sinners in hell, but he didn't hit me, though it would have been the most natural thing for him to do, and when I put him down in the backseat of the Friendlytown Lady's van, he clasped his arms around my neck and wouldn't let go. A few days later, he was sent home to his mother, and if part of me was sick with guilt and pity, the greater part was relieved.

During the entire showdown on the stairs, I don't recall seeing a single cat, not even Bitey, who was pretty much fearless. They were all hiding.

This wasn't the end of our relationship with Wilfredo. Six years later, at the top of those same stairs, he'd announce that he was gonna cut off my nuts, and I'd tell him that if he kept that up, I was gonna stuff him in the fucking car and drive him down to Brooklyn and drop him off on his mother's doorstep, I didn't care if it was two in the goddamn morning, I'm sure she'd be happy to see him. Wilfredo was joking about cutting my nuts off, but I was serious about taking him back to his mother's. My voice was raw, my face red and sweaty. He didn't keep it up, and we got through the rest of the summer without incident. Though, come to think of it, it was the last summer he spent with us.

Still, I sometimes think of the earlier moment, the moment we sent him away, as the beginning of F.'s and my rupture. Not the act—we were in that together—but the feelings afterward.

4

BY THE EVENING OF SEPTEMBER 30, BRUNO STILL hadn't called or e-mailed. I returned to the discount airline's website and selected a Thursday flight to La Guardia. How irritating that they wouldn't let the traveler type in dates but forced him to click boxes on a calendar! Was the airline trying to attract illiterate flyers? Did I want to fly on such an airline? Once more, I hesitated. I checked the balances in my bank accounts; they were no higher than they'd been that morning. I'd have to put it on credit. I tried Skyping F. at her residency, and again no one picked up. I wondered if she was avoiding me. She'd been distant lately. Biscuit had now been gone three days. By the time I arrived in New York, it'd be five. What were the chances that she'd still be hanging around the house after all that time? And if she hadn't come back to a place that she associated with food and warmth, how likely was she to come back just because she heard me calling her? Where a cat is concerned, you can't really speak of its master's voice. My friend Jo Ann, who knows more about animals than I do, thought Biscuit might have gone out to look for me, the human who'd cared for her and then gone away. That seemed especially terrible. It was as if I'd lured her from safety, to what might easily be her death. The more I thought about it, the more certain I became that she was dead. Why fly seven hundred miles to look for something you know is dead?

Later, I got an e-mail from F. She reminded me that Biscuit was a very smart, experienced cat who'd lived in our house for over a year, not a sick little kitten who'd been there only a couple of months. The last part of the sentence held a note of reproach — what was I getting my drawers in a twist for? Still, overall, it was as close as F. ever comes to optimism. Her optimism seemed a little heartless to me, but in the past, I knew, there'd been times when my optimism had seemed heartless to her, and so I accepted it. Sometimes all you want is for someone to tell you it will be all right, even if you know better.

~ ~ ~

We began letting Biscuit out of the house a month or two after we had her spayed. At first it was just for a little while, and we kept checking on her to make sure she didn't wander off. "Biscuit, Biscuit, Biscuit!" one or the other of us would yell from the doorstep, always three times, as in a fairy tale, and watch with pleasure as she scampered over to us. Some of that pleasure was relief that she was still there, and some of it was inspired by her compliance (she became less compliant as she got older). And it was pleasing to see that Biscuit already recognized her name. I doubt she recognized it in the sense that Augustine remembers recognizing, as a young child, that particular sounds, which he did not yet understand to be words, stood for particular things: "When people gave a name to an object and when, following the sound, they moved their body toward that object, I would see and retain the fact that that object received from them this sound, which they pronounced when they intended to draw attention to it." More likely she recognized it as a vocalization of the same kind as the ones she'd learned earlier from her mother, or perhaps had been born knowing. John Bradshaw and Charlotte Cameron-Beaumont identify some of these below:

Name	Typical duration (s)	Fundamental pitch (Hz)	Circumstances
Purr	2+	25–30	Contact
Trill/chirrup	0.4–0.7	250–800	Greeting, kitten contact
Miaow	0.5–1.5	700–800	Greeting
Female call	0.5–1.5	?	Sexual
Mowl (male call)	?	?	Sexual
Howl	0.8–1.5	700	Aggressive
Growl	0.5–4	100–225	Aggressive
Yowl	3–10	200–600	Aggressive
Snarl	0.5–0.8	225–250	Aggressive
Hiss	0.6–1.0	Atonal	Defensive
Spit	0.02	Atonal	Defensive
Pain shriek	1–2.5	900	Fear/pain

One is struck by how many of these sounds are related to aggression.

Augustine's famous account of how he learned language treats words as signs that refer to objects in the real world, that is, the mute world of things that we think of as the real one. In this account, a word's chief function is to point beyond itself, like a finger that directs your gaze to the horizon, where some trees are standing. Another word for this pointing operation is meaning. To ask what a word means is to ask what it points to. It may point narrowly, designating one tree and not another, this ash, not that maple. We call this denotation. The word may point more broadly, at the entire forest. Maybe the pointing hand opens to take in the sinking sun, the lengthening shadows of trunks and branches, which farther in thicken into a second wood, a wood within the wood, or beneath it, made up not of matter but of shadow. That is connotation. In the middle of the passage of our life, I found myself in a dark wood. But try pointing out something to a cat sometime. It won't look where you're pointing. It will look at your finger; it may rub against it. The cat represents a limit case of semiotics. The sounds it makes don't point to anything. Inasmuch as they serve mainly to express feeling or elicit behavior from the hearer, those sounds might be said to press buttons. A cat meows to be fed, to be let in from the cold or out into it. It yowls to give vent to its rage and intimidate another cat or any animal that's susceptible to being intimidated. I've seen a video of a cat yowling at a bear, and then chasing it as it flees. To Biscuit, "Biscuit," didn't "stand for" anything. It summoned her, as a bell might, and probably a lot of its effectiveness had to do with the way we said "Biscuit," or sang it, in a high voice that rose on the first syllable and dropped on the second, the combination of rising and falling tones being almost the same as that in a meow. To Biscuit, "Biscuit" wasn't a noun; it was a verb, one that took only the imperative mood, and at those increasingly frequent times she didn't come when we called her, one could say that the verb had become meaningless.

This isn't to say she was unresponsive. She was anything but. In no time she was famous for her friendliness. In the morning she'd make the rounds of the houses on the block, bustling from one to the next in her short-legged, bowlegged way, her tail erect. People would call to her from their gardens. She'd lie in wait on the front lawn for our neighbor Kathy's old beagle, whom she liked to taunt by stretching languorously on her side until the dog came straining toward her—his blunt, hoary muzzle twitching—then springing away at the last second. She might stroll over to the riding stable at the end of the street to visit the horses. A woman who worked there told me that she once saw Biscuit grab a horse's tail in both paws and swing from it like Tarzan. It was a miracle she didn't get her brains kicked out. F. and I were outsiders in the town, what the locals call "citiots," except we lived there full-time, and lacking children or a house of our own, we were cut off from the calm, self-important hum of town life. Biscuit was our emissary. She was what we talked with our neighbors about.

"Your cat was over," someone would greet us when we came home.

"She give you any trouble?"

"No, no, she couldn't have been sweeter. She's welcome any time."

We were happy then, and while it's stupid to make an animal the emblem of your happiness, I thought of Biscuit that way. Well, she was a happy cat. Even her busy, scissoring stride conveyed happiness, the purposeful happiness of someone going off to do something she loves. Watching her from the doorway, F. would sing bouncily in time with her gait: "Na-na-na-na-na-na-NAH, na-na-na-nah-nah-NAH!" She was going out into the world to be happy, and the world would oblige her, offering her its mice and birds, protecting her from speeding cars (we lived on a cul de sac) and villainous dogs (the town had a leash law).

What that world was for her, it was for us, mostly. Several nights a week we'd walk down the quiet street past our neighbors' houses, where TVs spilled their aquarium glow onto tidy mats of lawn. In the warm months, we'd head west onto Astor Road; we liked to bike there during the day. At night, the road rose and fell steeply amid groves of oaks and maples whose trunks shone a necrotic greenish-white beneath the moon. Between the trees, you could see the lighted windows of rich people's houses, which might have been welcoming if they hadn't been set so far back in the woods. Walking unseen through this dreaming landscape seemed to stimulate F. It amplified her sense of herself as an invisible outsider, and at the same time gave her a pretext for feeling like one, because of course anyone who walks out by night will be invisible to those who stay inside, which outside cities is almost everybody. As a teenager in a Midwestern suburb, F. used to creep out of the house after dark to spy on her family members. One time, she told me, she'd shinnied onto the roof and looked in on her father as he sat reading in his study. What she saw on these expeditions wasn't radically different from what she saw in the house during the day. Nobody shot dope or beat off to porn or wept over old love letters. They were just themselves, though sometimes they weren't. She remembered the thoughtful way her father had taken a nut from a can balanced on the arm of his chair and looked at it appraisingly before putting it in his mouth. She remembered moments when familiar faces went dead, so that the animated voices that issued from them seemed to be the voices of indwelling spirits or demons. F. half believes in demons.

Walking by night frightened F. too—who can walk through the woods at night without being a little frightened?—but that was its own kind of stimulus. Every so often we'd see the headlights of an approaching car and crowd onto the shoulder. Once, as the glare licked up the asphalt toward us, F. stuck her arms out rigidly before her and rolled up her eyes. She's a pretty woman, even a beautiful one, but she can make horrible faces; it may be her prettiness that makes them horrible. Her eyes pop, her white teeth flash with carniverous mirth. At that moment, she might have been the Platonic archetype of a zombie, minus the decay. I stuck my arms out too, and we shuffled along like that into the oncoming lights, wishing we could see the look on the driver's face. Afterward I marveled that he hadn't run us over.

When it got colder, we took a different route and crossed the main street into an immigrant neighborhood of flimsy bungalows with two families sardined inside, or, more often, half a dozen lonely men. They'd come up to pick apples or berries or do construction at low wages and stayed on, indispensible and resented. One night we passed a tent where a party was going on, swooning accordions, the sweet bray of horns. It was late fall and chilly, but the celebrants stood outside, drinking from bottles of beer. They were small, stolid people who didn't smile much, and then only shyly, baring the fugitive glint of gold teeth. Under their work coats, the men wore clean white shirts, the women, dresses in hot reds and greens. Their shyness passed to us. We said hello but little more. We didn't ask them what they were celebrating. To me, it looked like a wedding, and I would have said, "Felizidad," if I hadn't been afraid it would sound condescending. They might just have been partying for the hell of it.

The first time I realized I wanted to marry F., I shrank back in dismay. We'd only been seeing each other six months. What was six months? My therapist said it was half a year. I said that couldn't be healthy. Well, what did I think was healthy? In the moment he uttered it, the word "healthy" became moronic: a brussels sprout was healthy. I said I didn't know. Shouldn't I get to know F. better? I don't remember his answer. Being a therapist, and one who'd been analytically trained, he probably asked me another question. I was so afraid of being wrong; I'd been afraid most of my life. Whenever I'd broken up with someone, it was because I was scared I was making a mistake, and if I hadn't actually fallen out of love with her, I could foresee a time when I would, like the dim halo that wavers in the darkness of a country road at night, obscured by a curve in the road, that in another moment brightens into the doom of on-coming headlights. And what happens then? my shrink may have asked, meaning, I suppose, what happens if you fall out of love with her? Thinking of F., I would have said, Then I'll still be interested in her, because I already knew that to be true; she would hold my interest. But I'm still thinking of my metaphor, the one of headlights, because the answer that comes to me — not then, but now, at this moment — is, Then we crash.

A few weeks later, I went to the safety deposit at my bank and, after checking my box out of the vault, took it into one of the closets where people pore over their valuables, some gloat-ingly, some fretfully, the way my mother used to, muttering the names of her holdings to make sure every certificate was still there, some in despair at how little they have to their name, a few documents engraved with allegorical goddesses, jewelry nobody wants to wear, some old coins from a country that no longer exists. My box didn't have much in it. I took out a smaller — a very small — box, covered in blue velvet, and opened it a crack, out of the exaggerated caution that some-times comes over me as if to make up for the years I spent walk-ing around with my money in my hands, looking for someone to give it to for nothing. I snapped the box shut, put it in my shoulder bag, and then transferred it to my trouser pocket, one of the front ones. By the time I was walking out of the bank, I'd begun to worry that the box was making a bulge, but I could hardly take it out in the middle of a street in lower Manhattan, which at the time was not yet so rich that there was nothing you could possibly take out of your pocket that anybody in the vicinity would want because everybody already had more of it than you did. Though I guess someone still might take it from you out of greed, for which there is always a more beyond more, or spite.

Inside the box was my mother's engagement ring, a modest but very clear diamond set between two sapphires. It had come to me when she died three years before. I'd decided to take the ring up to the country the next day and present it to F. at the right moment, trusting that the moment's rightness would be revealed to me before it passed. It would be only the second time in my life that I'd proposed to someone, and the first time, seventeen years before, had been mostly out of guilt because she'd so plainly wanted to be proposed to and everything else I'd given her had been so shoddy and so quickly reneged on. That morning I laid out the jewel box beside my overnight bag along with some clothes and toiletries, then left the apartment to discharge my nervous energy working out. It was late summer; the pavements shimmered. When I came back from exercising, I was sweaty and sore, but I no longer felt like vomiting. I had an hour and a half before my train. That seemed like enough time. I showered and packed; I made myself a cup of coffee. I filled the cats' bowls with two days' worth of food and water and turned on a fan for them. Then I got ready to leave. All I had to do was put the box in my pocket. I'd decided that would be the safest place to keep it and had solved the bulge problem by putting on a pair of cargo shorts with pockets so deep I could have carried a .44 in one without anybody knowing. The pockets, moreover, snapped shut. But the ring wasn't where I'd left it on the bed. I thought I might have moved it to the nightstand, but it wasn't there either. It wasn't in the drawer of the nightstand. Could I already have slipped it in a pocket and forgotten? I patted them down like a TSA agent and turned them inside out for good measure. They were empty. I hadn't taken the ring into the bathroom when I showered—at least I didn't see it on the counter or the sink or on top of the toilet tank, which would have been a really stupid place to put a diamond ring, considering how easily one of the cats might jump up and knock it into the bowl. I hadn't taken it down to the kitchen when I'd made coffee; I looked there too. I looked inside the refrigerator.

I was sweating now, worse than I had while skating along the Hudson; my armpits were sour and dank. Every breath held the threat of a sob. I revisited places I'd searched only minutes before; it was like some awful dream of loss. At one point, finding another drawer or cupboard empty, I bellowed and flung my coffee cup at the wall. An explosion of black liquid and white shards. The cats, who'd been following me closely, ran.

In another minute, I'd either have to cancel my reservation or go to F. ringless. Looking back, I see that neither would have been a big deal. There were plenty of other trains, and she had no idea of what I was planning to offer her. At the time, though, it seemed that my whole fate was at stake, that if I didn't give F. the ring now, I never would, and sooner or later we would pass out of each other's lives forever. I fell to my knees at the foot of the bed and dropped my face into my hands. "Tell me what to do," I said. Maybe it was just, "What do I do?" I don't know what I said. I don't know what I was speaking to. Nothing spoke back to me.

I got up. The bed stretched below me like a landing strip, with the overnight bag at its center. Just beyond the bag, in its shadow, so to speak, was the small blue velvet box with my mother's ring inside it. Trust me, I checked.

~~~

I file e-mails compulsively, and the moment an airline sends me confirmation of a flight, I usually place it in a folder marked "Subscriptions." But I can't find a confirmation for the flight I booked on the night of September 30 and so don't know for sure what time I finally made my reservation. At around 7:15, it appears, I changed my password, since the airline sent me a message to that effect. I must have forgotten my old one. Why anybody should need a password to book a trip on a fucking airplane is beyond me. I can all too clearly picture myself typing different combinations of letters and numbers in the designated space and having each one rejected, my anger mounting like the anger of a sucker in Vegas feeding quarters into an unresponsive slot machine, or maybe what the sucker really feels is dread. I picture myself cursing with unproductive monotony, quite possibly weeping—a strangled cry of "I can't, I can't!"—and at last clicking "Forgot your password?" which, no matter what the intention behind it, always seems like a taunt. There would have been a wait. The airline's reply is time-stamped 7:17, and I must have followed up at once, fearing that if I didn't, I might forget the new password too; I wouldn't put it past myself. So let's say I booked my flight between 7:18 and 8:00.

Why is it so important for me to know? Maybe because the facts of my life seem less certain to me when I am alone, less facts than suppositions. Whatever the state of your feelings for each other, a spouse is a witness. She can tell you if you're walking around with toothpaste on your shirt (usually, she will). She can tell you if you brought the dry cleaning home and what you had for dinner. A cat is also a witness, although a silent one. Even at those times when I've gone days without seeing another human being, I've always been conscious that my cats are nearby and that they are watching me. Every time I rise from my desk, one is looking up at me from its resting place by the printer. On entering the living room, I pass the chair where another one is sitting and feel its gaze on me. Late at night, when I wake with a gasp from a bad dream, it's to find a cat peering at me, its eyes glowing faintly in the moonlight that streams through the shades. And because they are watching, my actions—and maybe even my thoughts—register on me in a way they otherwise might not. They have enough weight and gravity for me to remember them later.

But at that time and place, I had no witness.

What did I do the rest of that night? I wrote e-mails. I read, or tried to read, my undergraduates' essays. One of them began with a description of a small object falling out of the sky and landing at the writer's feet. Only when it was lying there did she recognize it as an injured hummingbird. A moment later, it died.

~ ~ ~

It's hard to get a cat to do tricks. The difficulty and the reluctance responsible for it are often cited in debates on feline intelligence, mostly by skeptics. In one study, in which subjects could get food by pressing a lever on a kind of vending machine, cats performed worse than pigeons. For a long time one of the least-used books in my library was *Tricks Your Cat Can Do*. Somebody gave it to me as a gift back when I first had Bitey, and I tried it out for a month or two before exiling it to a series of remote bookshelves, for I kept taking it with me when I moved, out of hope or habit, periodically bringing it out to gaze at its photos of cats jumping onto their owners' shoulders or tapping the keys of a piano. Fifteen years and four moves later, I finally got rid of it in a yard sale.

Still, there's a trick I managed to teach Biscuit. She liked being petted and, in her eagerness for affection, would practically butt against my hand. If, while petting her, I lowered my face to her level, she'd rub against it, cheek against cheek. She'd do it over and over. At close range, her face was a tawny, shield-shaped blur, paler at the muzzle and cheeks. Her breath was musty but not unpleasant, smelling of the dry nuggets I poured into her bowl every morning, a scent of dried fish and, oddly, leather, as if from a saddlery. Her gold-green eyes, which usually had some discharge at their corners, were intent but not especially loving. I don't know if you can see love in a cat's eyes the way you can in a dog's, and of course dogs turn their amorous gaze on everybody and everything, down to the half-eaten burger somebody dropped in the grass two nights ago that they regard as if it were an old, dear friend before snapping it up. Sometimes it occurs to me that what I saw as I rubbed faces with Biscuit wasn't much different from what a mouse might see in the moment before she punched its little ticket. In my case, though, she was purring.

As tricks go, it's not very impressive. All I did was encourage Biscuit to do what she'd do anyway, rub against me when I petted her, just substituting my face for my hand. This is said to be the fundamental rule of training any animal: you can only get it to do what it wants to do—in essentialist terms, to act in accordance with its nature. If I were more ambitious, I could have trained her to respond to a verbal cue. The thing would be to start out by petting her, I guess, and then to say, "Give me some love," or something equally gross and present my face for her to butt against. In the beginning I'd probably have had to say it over and over—"Gimme some love, gimme some love"—like a Barry White song. In time, she might have come to respond to the words alone. This would be a classic example of forward conditioning, in which a stimulus—here, the words "Gimme some love"—brings on a response (i.e., rubbing).

My projections of success may be rosy, since Biscuit's response to other words was hit-or-miss. She didn't always come when we called her name, and barking "no!" wasn't always enough to stop her from misbehaving. It wasn't the time she brought in that chipmunk. The one cue that almost always worked was the call "meaty dinner!" But of course the conditioned, verbal stimulus was reinforced by other stimuli, both conditioned and unconditioned, since F. or I sang out the words at the same time of day, and when Biscuit raced into the house or pattered downstairs from one of her sleeping spots, an unconditioned stimulus in the form of a dish of canned food was waiting for her. This was the thing she wanted, the thing for which all other stimuli, temporal or verbal, were only signs, or perhaps, given the animal's confusion of contingency and cause, means. The cry "meaty dinner!" and the fading light weren't indications that food was ready. They were what made food happen. And it was food she loved.

But then, why do cats do so badly in those learning experiments? If they love food, why can't they figure out that pushing a particular lever will make it come rattling down into a dish? I can't believe it's because they're stupid. The psychologist Edward Thorndike placed cats in specially designed boxes from which they could escape by performing simple actions— pulling a loop of cord or stepping on a platform or pushing a lever. The cats were kept hungry. Outside the box but in plain sight of the captives, the experimenter left some food. He found that certain cats, by trial and error, learned how to break out of their traps and get at the food. With repetition, they were able to do it in no time at all, having formed, as Thorndike put it, "a perfect association between the sense-impression of the interior of the box and the impulse leading to the successful movement." Cats, in other words, are bad at getting food from a vending machine but excellent at getting out of a box in order to feed themselves. It may be that, after millions of years of feeding not on stationery nuts and seeds but on clever, fast-moving birds and rodents, cats are poorly adapted to the monotony of pressing a lever to secure a few pellets—the portions in the experiment are pretty chintzy—of dry food. It may be that in the hierarchy of feline skills, extraction ranks lower than escape.

According to a study that sifted through DNA samples collected from 979 house cats and wildcats on three continents—
the collecting can't have been much fun—the domestic cat is
descended from *Felis silvestris lybica,* the Near Eastern wildcat
found in the deserts of Israel and the Arabian Peninsula. Some
12,000 years ago, this creature is thought to have taken up
habitation in the early agricultural settlements of the Fertile
Crescent. At first, the wildcats probably just darted in long
enough to snatch a few rats from the granaries, but over time
they began staying longer. The farmers must have welcomed
the small, deft creatures that silently prowled their storehouses,
stalking the vermin that ravaged the wheat and barley. It
helped that the visitors were unobtrusive. They made no claim
on their hosts. They wanted nothing but the pests they hunted
with such artful dedication, lying in wait for them in the shadows, their sleek bodies flattened to the earth, their eyes full of
light, their pupils like black suns. Their cruelty was marvelous.
How they toyed with their prey, pinning it down only to let it
wriggle free so they could pounce on it again; they'd do it over
and over until their victim died of terror or exhaustion.

Thousands of years later, in "Jubilate Agno," Christopher
Smart would ascribe these habits to chivalry:

For when he takes his prey he plays with it to give it a
chance.
For one mouse in seven escapes by his dallying.

But chivalry was only invented in the Middle Ages, most
peoples up until then having commonsensically believed that

there was no point in showing mercy to a helpless enemy unless you meant to make him a slave. And Smart wrote "Jubilate Agno" in the madhouse.

Certainly, the cats must have had to modify their behavior. They learned not to snarl and strike out at the large creatures whose dens so abounded in game and not to shit in the dried grass seeds they liked to eat. In this way, they became the first animals to domesticate themselves. The adaptation probably took place through the same trial-and-error process by which Thorndike's cats learned to escape traps, except it wasn't just individuals that were adapting but an entire species, or the progenitors of one. Tests of mitochondrial DNA indicate that all of today's house cats are descended from five female lineages, five feline Eves.

It makes sense that cats and humans would learn to live together. Each had something the other needed. The mystery is when their relation evolved beyond convenience. Did one of the visitors grow so used to the great creatures that one day he forgot himself and brushed against one as he might brush against one of his own kind, except that instead of a flank he was making contact with an enormous leg? He may have meant nothing by it, just wanted to stamp the other creature as being, briefly, his. (Cats are possessive, but only on a short-term basis, judging by the way different individuals in a household will rub in turn against the same door frame in passing, as though punching a factory clock, with no cat appearing to take umbrage at later claimants.) Did the cat purr as it did this? And did the great creature, sensing its intent or just enjoying the supple, furry caress, reach down and stroke the little creature in return? Imagine how clumsy he must have been, his hand stiff as a paddle. Children always have to be taught how to stroke a cat rather than thump it like a dog. "Don't *pat* her, *pet* her," I remember telling Wilfredo. He looked at me narrowly, wondering what he was doing wrong and maybe, given things I learned later, if I was going to hit him. It's possible that the first such exchange was between a cat and a human child. The difference in their sizes wouldn't have been that great, and cats, like other mammals, seem able to recognize the young of other species, thanks to their large round heads and eyes and small mouths and noses, the same features that make kittens so appealing.

Call this the simple friendliness that arises between individuals when they share an environment in a mutually beneficial way. You see it in offices. Such friendliness is pragmatic, acknowledging the services the parties render each other and building up a fund of good will against future conflicts, as for instance when one party defecates in the other's food supply or thoughtlessly steps on the other's tail. At those times I hurt Biscuit by accident, eliciting a pain shriek whose real duration may have been between one and two and a half seconds but that seemed to go on forever, I was always touched when, after an interval of brooding under a bed, she allowed me to pet her again. "I'm sorry, sweetheart," I'd tell her and reach down to scratch her head, which astonishingly rose to meet my hand, and I marveled at the trust she showed for a creature that a little while before had caused her to scream in pain and that by sheer virtue of its size could easily kill her.

Some 9,500 years ago, on the island of Cyprus, in a village called Shillourokambos, a man was buried beside a cat. A team of French archaeologists unearthed their bodies in 2001. Both sets of remains were well preserved, and although each had a separate grave, these were only sixteen inches apart and had been dug at the same time. Both man and cat lay with their heads facing west, the man with his arms crossed on his chest, the cat with its limbs tucked beneath it. The deceased man was about thirty and, judging by some shaped flints and a small green stone axe arrayed around him, a person of rank. The cat was only eight months old. It may have been killed to keep the man company in the grave or in whatever world the people of that time believed lay beyond it. While a nearby grave pit contained parts of several animals, the cat had been buried whole and intact in a way the scientists believed called attention to it as an individual. This creature and not another. With this man.

What happened between the time humans began admitting *Felis silvestris lybica* into their granaries (though, really, how could they have kept them out?) and the time they first took *Felis silvestris catus* with them into the afterworld?

Just before F. and I became lovers, I hung back. It was true I wanted her very much. She was the only person in any room in which I happened to find myself; whole cocktail parties were depopulated because of her. And I didn't want to be in any room that didn't have her in it. The trouble was that by then I also liked her. I hadn't thought that would happen. How had the woman who'd looked at me like I was a turd turned into somebody I liked? We were in a room in the city, high above the street. The lights were dim. The walls were hung with photographs that seemed to be portraits, but it was hard to tell. Were those shadows the faces of men or women? Were they faces at all? The lights in the street below might have been stars, each with its radiant smeared corona. I had to force myself to look at F. It was as if I were about to tell her something terrible. "I want you," was how I may have put it, "but I like having you as my friend. You're so nice. I'm just scared that if we go any farther, it'll fuck everything up."

I don't remember her answer, only how she looked at me, somberly and with such prolonged stillness that when she blinked it seemed as deliberate as a hand clap. Then, suddenly, breathtakingly, she smiled. In every account I give of her, there is always some indeterminacy, like the one in

Heisenberg's theory, which tells us that we can know where a thing is but not where it came from or where it's going. I can say how she looked but not what she said; I can call up her expression but not her words. Always something is veiled.

Proust was aware of this, as he was of so much else:

> The questing, anxious, exacting way we have of looking at the person we love, our eagerness for the word which will give us or take from us the hope of an appointment for the morrow, and, until that word is uttered, our alternate if not simultaneous imaginings of joy and despair, all this makes our attention in the presence of the beloved too tremulous to be able to carry away a very clear impression of her. . . . The beloved model does not stay still; and our mental photographs of it are always blurred.

Could I have looked forward from that moment to this one? We live in the country now, and our bedrooms are on the ground floor of the house. At night, the lights of passing cars sweep across the windows and render their curtains briefly transparent, turning them into colored scrims on which there flash glimpses of leafy branches in summer, bare ones in winter, the shadows of the kids from the nearby college as they parade up and down our road, talking in the loud, important voices of the young. Sometimes we're roused by drunken laughter. It drives F. crazy.

Another thing she hates is how exposed the house is. It makes her feel that she's an item in a display case, the case being located in a boutique for sex murderers. She has reasons for feeling this way; I imagine most women do. Our tall front windows look across a road onto an open field that rolls and dips past student dorms and parking lots to a gleaming performing arts space that from the outside might be a radio telescope canted at the stars. F. once had me go outside at night and walk partway across the field to see if she'd be visible to someone lurking there in the dark. I did as she asked. I skirted a small pond that glinted beneath the moon, climbed a rise, then picked my way down a shallow slope where some months later I would spot a small gray cat that I'd call to plaintively, futilely, the way you call out to a dead loved one in a dream, knowing he will not hear you. A little farther, I turned. The lights in the house were on, and I could see F. through the curtains, a small woman with silvery blonde hair looking out tensely into the night. I hesitated before coming back in, not knowing what to tell her. If I said I'd seen her, it would confirm her fears and she'd want to move; she wanted to move already. If I lied, I might lull her into a false sense of security in which she'd fail to notice the approach of a psycho with a knife. Besides, I'd be lying to her, and at that time I could still say I'd never lied to her, except maybe about how much ice cream was left in the carton in the freezer or what I'd thought of when exchanging looks with the photographer of faded rock stars, and that was a lie of omission. Besides, she wouldn't believe me.

On reentering, I told F. that I could see her, but only indistinctly, because of the curtains. She was recognizable as a woman, no doubt about it, but it was impossible to really say what she looked like or even how old she was. She might, I told her, have been an old woman.

F. said there were men who raped and murdered old women. She looked at me coldly. They specialized in them. How blue her eyes were!

Back when I lived in Baltimore, Bitey and I used to take walks together. I felt safe letting her out, knowing she'd keep to the alley that ran behind my street, which was too narrow for cars to drive down except in the most moseying way. The alley accommodated an entire ecosystem of cats, dozens of them, and the uncounted small creatures they preyed on. Bitey and Ching used to spend most of the day out there, sunbathing and strolling and exchanging mostly friendly greetings with their peers, except for a small, round calico who launched herself at any cat that so much as stuck its head into her yard and once chased Bitey halfway down the alley, claws extended and every hair erect, so that seen from above my cat seemed to be fleeing a small orange-and-white cannonball hurtling lethally a half foot above the ground. It was one of the few times I saw her afraid of anything.

Two or three nights a week, I'd visit a woman who lived a few blocks away. She wasn't a girlfriend, at least I never called her that and I doubt she ever spoke of me as her boyfriend: she was just someone I was seeing. I'd walk over there around ten. On seeing me getting ready to leave, Bitey would spring down from the sofa, stretch with purpose, and trot over to the door, her tail upright and undulant. We'd leave the house together; together we'd walk down the street to my date. I use "together" loosely. Sometimes she'd walk at my side; at others, she'd quicken her pace and stride ahead, stopping from time to time

to groom herself and, if you ask me, make sure I was still following her. The grooming always seemed pretextual, as it
would if a person walking briskly down a city street were to stop
without warning to ostentatiously comb her hair. My cat might
have been one of the touts who throng the wharfs of steamy
port cities—Tangier, Rio, Nha Trang, Surabaya—offering to
steer sailors to a good time. Sometimes she'd cross to the other
side of the street but still keep pace with me, her leggy black
form lithe and alert. Her strides were longer than Biscuit's, and
her shoulders had a confident roll, as if she'd never run from a
butterball of a calico. When I turned into my friend's walkway,
she'd keep going or loop back in the direction of our house.

But when I left three or four hours later, she was waiting for
me. Usually, she'd be lying in a bed of pachysandra, almost invisible except for the topaz flares of her eyes. "Well, hi there,"
I'd say. She'd walk up to me and sit, then raise her head to be
petted. Only when I had done this would she rise and accom-
pany me back to the house. In contrast to her earlier zigzag
progress, she now kept to my side. It was as if she were chaper-
oning me. Maybe Bitey, too, saw me as a deputy kitten. Like
Biscuit, she liked to groom me, but after a while of this her
pupils would widen abruptly. Her claws would come out and
pin the hand she'd been licking. If I tried pulling away, she'd
sink her fangs into the fleshy part, glaring up at me like
Richard III contemplating Clarence and wondering how he'd
fit in a butt of Malmsey. The only way to dislodge her was to
give her a tap on the nose—the same thing you're supposed to
do to an attacking pit bull, only more forcefully—or let the
hand remain limp until she was persuaded it was dead. None

of that wildness was on view during our predawn walks. The streets were empty. The city's crime lights, which did nothing to prevent crime, turned the sky a velvety mauve. In the shadows of the trees, frogs were peeping; a rat poked its head out of a storm drain. Bitey registered them disinterestedly, the way a human might, as if they were phenomena of a nature to which she wasn't completely subject, for isn't that how humans think of nature? Once upon a time we were figures in its landscape, but now we have stepped out and look back at it with a proprietary eye, thinking, How lovely! or, Somebody ought to clear those pines.

I didn't show F. the ring till late the next morning. We were in her bedroom. A shaft of sunlight fell through the window, highlighting the rose tint of her skin, the roundness of her arms and breasts. "I want to show you something." I rolled out of bed and went over to where my shorts lay tangled and drew the jewel box from an enormous pocket. Looking back, I'm startled to think I left a thing of such value in a pair of shorts I'd torn off like some hated bondage and left overnight on the floor, where a cat had sat on them, leaving some of its hair. I must have crawled back to the bed, because when I held out the box to F. I was sitting below her, or maybe kneeling, the way you're supposed to, and it seems unlikely that I would have walked over and then lowered myself. It would have been very awkward.

When I showed her the box, she seemed embarrassed. For a moment, I was afraid she was embarrassed for me. I might have put the box back in my pants if there'd been a graceful way to do it, I mean both physically—I couldn't turn and crawl back the way I'd come without displaying my ass—and emotionally. To get both of us off the hook, I said, "I'd like to marry you, but I'm not sure I want to live together." I meant it too. It had been twelve years since I'd last lived with a woman, and I was used to being by myself.

She may have been hurt. She may have been relieved. I remember her smiling broadly, hugely. It had been more than twenty years since she'd lived with a man. Both of us liked sex and were prone to brief, free-falling infatuations we then spent months feeling shitty about, years. The fools we'd made of ourselves, to say nothing of others. When did it become standard practice to pretend you didn't really want the person you were ready to cut out your heart for? The Greeks knew nothing of this.

She may have asked me if I was proposing, wanting clarification.

I said I was. I was proposing to her. Would she marry me?

After a while, she said yes.

For hundreds of years before the invention of dating, taking a walk was one of the few things a young man could acceptably ask a girl he liked to do with him.

Would you like to go out walking with me, Miss Alice? Walking allowed the young people to spend time together free from the surveillance of the girl's family, though someone—a vigilant little brother—might be delegated to follow at a distance to keep an eye on things. Walking gave the boy and girl something to do apart from exchange gasped politenesses in the parlor. It gave them topics of conversation. The wheat's coming up high this year. Isn't that a splendid cloud! Are you fond of birdsong, Mr. Lane? It much depends on the bird. Of course. What do you think of the lark? I should say the lark has a most melodious song. A drawback of stationary, indoor courtship was that it required the actors to *look at* each other without staring, which would be rude, or make too great a show of *not* staring, which would be just as rude and appear shifty besides. When walking, however, they had perforce to pay attention to the road before them, since otherwise they might tumble into a ditch, and this gave them some respite from the labor of unceasing mutual scrutiny. They inspected each other in sidelong glances. What they saw was mostly profile.

When I recall the walks I took with F.—still take, at rarer and rarer intervals—that is how I see her. Below the smooth arc of her high forehead, which seems to glow with intelligence and purpose, is the smaller arc of one blue eye, the sharp angle of her nose with its inquisitive pointed tip, the tiny, beveled notch, like the mark of a chisel, where her lips meet. With a little exaggeration, her profile might be the kind you used to see on matchbooks advertising correspondence schools of art.

We take walks in the city, of course, but it's in the country that I envision her, maybe because there's less there to distract me from her presence, which I am so aware of even when I'm not looking at her, as one is aware, even in pitch darkness, of the nearness of a body of water. Early in our relationship, walking with F. always made me a little anxious. She was so quiet, and I worried that I was talking too much or, if I didn't talk, which I could do if I put my mind to it, that she'd think I was just slavishly imitating her silence. I may or may not have looked at her too much, but I'm sure the way I looked at her was questing, anxious, exacting. As lovely as it was to me, I wasn't content to contemplate F.'s surface: I wanted to see beneath that surface. Back then, the main thing I wanted to see was what she thought of me, so I suppose my curiosity was like a bat's echolocation, that is, a way of finding out where I stood. Proust again:

> When we are in love, our love is too big a thing for us to be able altogether to contain it within ourselves. It radiates towards the loved one, finds there a surface which arrests it, forcing it to return to its starting-point, and it is this repercussion of our own feeling which we call the other's feelings and which charms us more then than in its outward journey because we do not recognize it as having originated in ourselves.

I still watch F. while we walk, and I still speculate about her inner life. But the content of those speculations has changed. I— I mean the mostly imaginary being F. may have an opinion of—have mostly vanished from them. It's F. who interests me. She's an observant person, maybe the most observant person I know, and so I spend a lot of time wondering what she sees as we follow Astor Road or one of the other routes we've adopted since we moved out of the village. Which of those trees is she looking at? This ash or that maple? That oak whose arthritically gnarled trunk is so thick it would take three grown men to span it with their arms? Does she see those branches that crosshatch the sky like brushstrokes of some maniacally ornate calligraphy? Does she notice the birds on the horizon or the sunlight falling on the rock? Does she see the hinges of that fallen gate, which rust has turned into a row of orange *H*'s that burn against the gray of the weathered posts, and would she say the *H*'s stand for "Heaven" or "Hell"? From time to time, one of us will be so struck by some feature of the landscape that he or she has to point it out to the other. Usually, I try to do this without speaking. Some of that is deference to F.'s customary silence, but it's also a game, because along with wanting to know what F. sees, I want to know if she sees what I do. And so I point and wait for her to tell me.

I think back to those nights I walked with Bitey from my lover's house in Baltimore. (Strange that when I remember the woman I used to balk at calling my girlfriend, I now think of her as my lover.) I had lived with this creature for five years, longer than I'd lived with any human being since I was a child. I'd spent hours feeding her, petting her, playing with her. She had slept in my arms. I had seen her shitting; I had scooped her shit into a bag. And yet I had no idea what she thought— or, given our ignorance as to whether cats think at all, what transpired in her consciousness—as we walked the streets. The city's dreadful night would have been less dark to her than it was to me, since a cat's pupils can dilate much wider than a human's, and its retinae have more rods. She would have been extraordinarily attuned to small movements, a chipmunk rubbing its paws together in that supplicating way they have, a nuthatch cocking its head. And yet much of what she saw would be blurred and lacking in detail. The same optical features that give a cat night vision give it a more limited depth of field. Bitey couldn't tell red from green. Maybe she seemed so indifferent to those frogs because she couldn't see them. I had no way of knowing.

~ ~ ~

I've been reading some of the e-mails I wrote between the time I learned of Biscuit's disappearance on September 29 and flew to New York on October 2. I keep looking for some indication of what I was thinking back then: not what I was *feeling*—I can remember that all too well, in all its clamminess—but what was going on in the portion of my brain that's commonly portrayed as rational—what is that, the frontal lobe? That I cannot remember. I was half convinced that Biscuit was dead and half convinced that even if she was alive, she was unlikely to be anyplace where I could find her. I didn't want to spend money I didn't have traveling seven hundred miles to have my heart broken searching for a cat I wouldn't find. And yet I did. I went. What was I thinking?

"I don't know if my being there will accomplish anything," I wrote F. "By that time she'll have been gone 5 or 6 days, since

Bruno thinks the last time he saw her was Saturday *morning*. I could cut out his heart. But I don't know what else to do. If she's near enough to hear a human voice and sound enough to respond to it, it'll be mine."

To other correspondents, I wrote,

Like an idiot, I started bargaining with God the other night and announced that I'd be willing to lose everything else as long as I could have her back, or at least know she was safe and happy.

And:

I just know I won't be able to rest until we find her or are convinced she's dead, and I'd rather be up there doing something than sitting here brooding and cursing.

And:

If she's alive and somewhere near the house, she's more likely to respond to my voice than to Bruno's. It's stupid and sentimental, but she's the one thing or creature I can't bear to lose. Which may be a message that one must be prepared to lose everything.

Even now, I cringe at the melodrama of the last one. But I was upset and had barely slept for two nights. In the end, I think I just had to go. I mean, I didn't think. I *had* to go, as imperatively as I would have to pull my hand away from a hot stove, only more slowly and using a credit card. Otherwise, I couldn't live with myself.

~~~

Like just about everything else in the world, theories of love can be divided into two kinds. One view is that love requires knowledge, is predicated on it, and that you can only love—really love—somebody you know. The other view is that love and knowledge are inimical. Love requires mystery, uncertainty, indeterminacy, can exist only in the dim zone where two personalities cast their shadows. You can trace the first theory back to Plato, who has Diotima tell Socrates, "For wisdom is a most beautiful thing, and Love is of the beautiful; and therefore Love is also a philosopher: or lover of wisdom." This is in the *Symposium*, a discourse on love framed by an account of a drinking party. Another guest at this party describes love as the mutual recognition of two maimed beings who once made up a whole but were sheared apart in the primordial past. Since that time, they have sought each other: "And when one of them meets with his other half, the actual half of himself, whether he be a lover of youth or a lover of another sort, the pair are lost in an amazement of love and friendship and intimacy, and would not be out of the other's sight, as I may say, even for a moment." This idea is preserved in the expression "my other half," though of course we most often hear that expression used ironically, by nightclub comics holding forth on the wretchedness of marriage. The Vietnamese go Plato one better and call their spouses, whether husbands or wives, *minh*, "my self." Not my other self, but the only one, to be cloven from which is not just to be diminished but destroyed.

Yet classical mythology is full of stories about the blindness of love. Their protagonists fall for animals, for celestial objects, for their own watery reflections. How stupid they are. Love has made them stupid. (We should qualify this and note once more that love degrades only mortals in this fashion: the gods take whom they please, and if from time to time one of those unhappy objects eludes them by turning into an alder tree or, having been rashly endowed with the gift of immortality, shrivels to a feeble, mindless, undying husk, that's not *their* problem. "My bad," Apollo sighs, and strums a melancholy air on his lyre, in the Mixolydian mode.) Although Plato believes love can usher us toward wisdom, he knows that more often it tends the other way: "The irrational desire which overcomes the tendency of opinion towards right, and is led away to the enjoyment of beauty, and especially of personal beauty, by the desires which are her own kindred—that supreme desire, I say, which by leading conquers and by the force of passion is reinforced, from this very force, receiving a name, is called love."

Augustine is even more skeptical. He comes by his skepticism honestly, having experienced relations with two women, whom the editor of my edition of the *Confessions* refers to as "concubines," and an indeterminate number of prostitutes. All in all, it seems pretty mild, given his triple-X reputation. This is the saint who gives his name to the Augustine Fellowship, more widely known as Sex and Love Addicts Anonymous. But as any addict can tell you, the measure of the disease isn't how much you consume; it's how much you suffer. Augustine suffered, never more than when he was trying to kick: "Fettered by the flesh's morbid impulse and lethal sweetness, I dragged my chain, but was afraid to be free of it."

One could protest that he isn't talking about love but lust. Elsewhere in the *Confessions*, he writes movingly about the love he feels for his mother and male friends. But even that love seems to him inferior to the love of God, at best only a coarse approximation, at worst a treacherous distraction, as if one were to try driving cross-country solely by looking in the mirrors. It was a mirror, a natural one, that destroyed Narcissus. He died for love of what he saw in it:

> Let these transient things be the ground on which my soul praises you (Ps. 145; 2), "God creator of all." But let it not become stuck in them and glued to them with love through the physical senses. For these things pass along the path of things that lead to non-existence. They rend the soul with pestilential desires, for the soul loves to be in them and take its repose among the objects of its love. But in these things there is no point of rest; they lack permanence. They flee away and cannot be followed with the bodily senses.
>
> This alone I know: without you it is evil for me, not only in external things but within my own being, and all my abundance which is other than my God is mere indigence.

Augustine has many reasons for being suspicious of the physical objects of love, from their sticky hold on the senses to the fact that they change and pass away. But his wariness is also epistemological. What can I know about this pear, this woman? What can I know about my friend? What can I know about my own being, that dark wood I stumble through with outstretched arms? One of the things God has going for him is that, unlike those other phenomena, he can be known, in the depths of the soul. Of course we can only know him imperfectly, but how else would an imperfect being know a perfect one?

Unlike Augustine and Plato, Proust had no faith in invisible, unchanging essences. For him the visible is everything. Few writers have worked so hard to render it, down to the precise shades of hawthorn blossoms and asparagus. Never mind the way he unfolds successive views of Albertine as she and Marcel first kiss, as if his narrator were a spacecraft lowering itself toward the surface of a strange planet and recording each stage of the descent with a continual barrage of photographs, not just photos but X-rays and spectrographs, intent on capturing every wavelength of the object's emanations. The description of that kiss goes on for pages. What necessitates its obsessive thoroughness, apart from Proust's obsessive temperament, is the fact that the view of Albertine keeps *changing*. And this scene offers the reader, in compressed form, a vision of the entire *In Search of Lost Time*, in which an insatiable consciousness tries to retrieve the changeable, impermanent figures that once passed through its ambit before veering off into the cold vastness of age and death.

What can you know about an object that's always changing? Especially when it's an object you love. Desire dilates the pupils (long before Photoshop, ad agencies were enlarging those of the models in photo spreads to create the illusion that they wanted you). But dilated pupils are good only for seeing in the dark. In ordinary light, they're useless. Consider what it's like to drive home from an eye exam, squinting against the brightness that crashes down from the sky. Proust understood that every lover is similarly blinded, blinded not by the obscurity of the love object but by the luminosity of his own feeling:

> Faced with the thoughts, the actions of a woman whom we love, we are as completely at a loss as the world's first natural philosophers must have been, face to face with the phenomena of nature, before their science had been elaborated and had cast a ray of light over the unknown. Or, worse still, we are like a person in whose mind the law of causality barely exists, a person who would be incapable, therefore, of establishing a connection between one phenomenon and another and to whose eyes the spectacle of the world would appear as unstable as a dream.

We were in F.'s bedroom. Sun, rose-lit skin, the roundness of arms and breasts. "I want to show you something." I rolled out of bed and went over to where my shorts lay tangled and drew the jewel box from a pocket. The pants were covered with cat hair. No sooner had I kicked them off the night before than Suki, the older of her cats, had approached them, sniffed, and sat. She was still sitting on them when I woke. She was an undemonstrative creature, but she liked to claim pieces of my clothing, whether for my benefit or that of my cats, whose scent she must have smelled on me, I don't know. I must have crawled back to the bed, because when I held out the box to

F., I was sitting below her, or maybe kneeling, the way you're supposed to, and it seems unlikely that I would have walked over and then lowered myself again. It would have been very awkward.

On seeing the ring, she laughed. For all my efforts to husband my dignity, I must have looked ridiculous crawling naked across the floor and then kneeling before her, holding out a blue velvet box whose lid I'd snapped open to display the flashing thing inside. My expression was probably earnest and mortified. But F.'s laughter also had pleasure in it, and from this I took encouragement.

"Do you know what this is?" I asked her. She laughed harder, which made me start laughing too. I told her to stop, I was serious. "Look," I began, then forgot what I was about to say and finally settled for the short version.

She didn't laugh this time, but from her smile I was afraid she might start again at any moment. She looked like a Renoir nude, only smaller and more fit. She looked like Tinkerbelle. As a young woman, she had practiced martial arts; when we held each other, I could still feel the strength that had given her.

She smiled wider. Silently, I willed her not to laugh. Then she said, "Maybe."

5

CONSIDERING HOW ANXIOUS I WAS ABOUT BISCUIT, it troubles me to realize I didn't leave for New York until October 2. How could I wait that long? The word that comes to mind is "cavalier." When I look through my calendar, I'm reminded that I'd already missed a bunch of classes the month before, having taken off on two successive weeks to attend a panel and show Bruno around the house. So maybe I was scared to miss any more. This was my first full-time teaching gig after years on the job market, and I was grateful for it, probably abjectly grateful, in a lank, stooped, Bob Cratchity way. Everything else I'd wanted in life seemed to be slipping out of my grasp, and so I held on to my job as if I'd never heard the warnings about clinging to anything too tightly, though usually those warnings are tendered about things like riches or prestige and not, say, cats. Nobody warns you about clinging too tightly to a cat.

I drove to the airport in my landlords' car, which they'd thrown in with the house, a terrific deal, if you consider what I was paying. It was a battleship gray Thunderbird dating from the late eighties or early nineties, with a hood as long as a bowling alley. The T-bird was ponderous on turns, and the door was so heavy that it tended to swing back shut before I could get out. By the end of the year, my right leg would be covered with bruises. Still, it would get me down to Myrtle Beach. Once you passed over the bridge, a gray-green steel vertical-lift bridge whose riveted joints rasped beneath the tires, the road was straight and didn't have too much traffic. The country was flat. Loblolly pines grew on the roadside. There were housing developments and trailer parks and a gentleman's club that projected a simultaneous air of invitation and supernatural menace, like if I stopped for a quick lap dance, I'd be rolled and have the shit beat out of me and miss my flight and then learn that Biscuit had been run over by a truck while she was trying to cross the road back to the house.

I should add that I've never had a lap dance in my life.

~~~

Biscuit would follow me when I left the house, but not for very long. Her attention faltered. Something stirred in the weeds on the side of the road, and she'd lunge at it; it might be a vole or a twist tie from yesterday's trash—one was as good as the other. When we were still living in the village, she could be distracted by any neighbor who happened to be digging in her garden. She'd storm right over to see what was in those holes. Often she was seized by a sudden, furious compulsion to groom herself. The suddenness was almost spasmodic; at times it looked like she was going to tip over. Yet, like all cats, she was also a miracle of poise. Watching her, I marveled at the balletic rigor with which she held up a hind leg, the paw extended so that leg and paw formed the long side of a flawless 45-degree angle, while the rest of her remained heedlessly fixated on her butt. Sometimes I almost thought she might vanish into her butt, or maybe up it—as in that cartoon I loved when I was thirteen, whose caption reads, "Your problem is obvious."

To me, this tension between abruptness and poise seems an essential part of feline nature. If you accept Descartes's view of animals as natural automata, machines made of meat and fur, you can visualize a cat as an automaton programmed to shuffle at random among a variety of subroutines. The shuffling can appear jerky and without purpose. Why abandon a nice walk with one's person to torment a piece of plastic? Why break off investigating the fascinating sounds and smells of a June morning to start fiercely licking one's back fur? (One possible answer is that domestication has robbed the machine of its original purpose, and it's simply discharging the energy that once would have been consecrated to hunting and killing.) At the same time, individual routines have to be carried out perfectly: the hind leg angled just so during grooming, the toes fanned apart so that you can see the smooth, eraser-pink clefts between them; the forepaws tucked beneath the breast before resting; the prey seized and reprieved so many times before it can finally be dispatched.

In general, Biscuit had a shorter attention span than Bitey did and a milder disposition. Bitey was the cat who'd skulk all day outside poor Tina's door, rehearsing the woe she had in store for her, whereas I once saw Biscuit sitting amicably beside a field mouse in front of a bed of daffodils in the garden. They couldn't have been more than a foot apart. Even if cats have terrible depth of visual field, she must have been aware of the creature, and it of her, but they ignored each other like commuters on the subway gazing up with tender neutrality at the zitty, love-starved foreigners in the ads for Dr. Zizmor's dermatology practice. At length the mouse seemed to realize what it was sitting next to and began sidling toward the flower bed. Only then did Biscuit take notice of it or remember that it belonged to the category "prey." The fur on the back of her neck rose. Her whole being quivered with interest. In another moment she would have pounced on it, if I hadn't picked her up and carried her, squirming and hissing, into the barn. She was really pissed at me.

If someone asked me why I love Biscuit, I might cite her mildness, even though it may not have been mildness at all, judging by the many tiny corpses deposited on the porch, just forgetfulness. But I also loved Bitey, and there was nothing mild about her. Soon after F. and I moved in together, Bitey put her in the hospital. I was in the kitchen when I heard snarls at the foot of the stairs. Tina had gone down there, and my cat had cornered her in the front vestibule and was rearing above her in a gloating rage. I started at them, yelling. F. came out of her room and ran downstairs to break up the fight. I remember feeling tacitly reproached. The stairs were steep and covered in unctuous brown carpeting. As I watched from below, F.'s feet slid out from under her, she grabbed hold of the banister but continued to fall or slide, and her arm twisted grotesquely in its socket and went limp. She cried out. I raced up to her, shooing

cats out of my way. F. was lying on her back. She was conscious
but her face was white and shiny with sweat. She thought the
arm was dislocated. I told her to lie still while I called 911, but
she said she wanted to go to the bathroom; she was scared she
was going to be sick. Cautiously, I half-carried her upstairs. I
must have made a call then, though I have no memory of it, because a pair of EMTs showed up within minutes. Ambulances
come quickly in the country, as long as it's not a weekend
night when drunken teens roar up and down the roads looking
for trees to wrap themselves around. The stretcher was too
wide to fit through the bathroom door horizontally, so F. had
to be strapped to it and carried out at an angle. I walked beside
it as the EMTs trundled her to the ambulance, holding her
good hand. If Bitey had been anywhere in sight, I would have
leapt on her and shaken her like a rag, but all the noise must
have scared her into hiding, and I didn't see her again till one
or two in the morning, when I brought F. back from the hospital, her arm having popped back into its socket without any
help from the admitting doctor, who sent her home with nothing but a crummy blue sling that was shortly covered in cat
hair. Bitey was lying on the dining table on top of a heap of
mail, and she barely glanced up when I called her an evil shit.

Of course cats have no sense of good and evil. I doubt dogs do
either, but we're more inclined to think of them as moral creatures, or at least as ones susceptible to moral suasion, properly
backed up with a rolled-up newspaper. "Bad dog!" you yell,
and the dog hangs its head and looks at you the way a Gnostic
believed its ancestor looked at God on the day we provoked

him to invent death. The jury's out as to whether that look signifies remorse or fear. "Bad cat!" accomplishes nothing, unless
you really yell it, in which case the subject runs for cover.
None of your expiatory displays of guilt or shame, it just books.
Biscuit was in some ways a very human cat, by which I mean a
cat who responds to human cues, answering your call at least
some of the time and giving you a look of what seems like gratitude when you fill her saucer with milk, though maybe it's
really *approval*; you've figured out what she wanted from you.
But I never saw her express anything that remotely resembled
guilt. Like Bitey before her, she learned not to claw the stereo
speakers or start knocking things off the dresser early in the
morning, but her forbearance appeared to be entirely pragmatic, and at those times she forgot herself and stretched sen-
suously toward a speaker with outspread talons and I snapped,
"Biscuit!" she paused and looked at me. Somebody else might
have called her expression insouciant or defiant or even, because of how her whiskers bristled, belligerent, but to me it was
just blank. I'd pressed the "Biscuit!" button, which made her
come, but she was already here, and the tone was the tone of
"no," the button that made her stop. So what did I want?

It may be their inability to display remorse—really, their inability to comprehend what remorse might be—that caused
cats so much trouble in the Middle Ages. Probably their stealth
and night walking didn't help either. People thought of them
as the devil's creatures and persecuted them accordingly.
Those jolly, howling orgies of cat killing may in fact have been
autos-da-fé, though knowing human nature, it's more likely the
mobs just wanted an excuse to visit suffering on something

small and weak. At the same time they were torturing and burning cats, Europeans were also torturing and burning heretics, especially the Cathars of the Languedoc. (One imagines an English-accented voiceover on the History Channel: "Is it mere coincidence that 'Cathar' contains the word 'cat'?" Well, actually, yes, according to my dictionary, which traces "Cathar" to the Greek *katharoi*, "the pure ones.") The violence against Cathars was organized and genocidal and bore the imprimatur of a couple popes, who proclaimed the campaign against the heretics in Toulouse as much a crusade as the ones against the infidels in the Holy Land. By the mid-fourteenth century, some 500,000 Cathars had been slaughtered, along with an undetermined number of Catholics who had the misfortune to live in Cathar towns. (Asked how to tell one from the other, a commander of the crusaders said, "Caedite eos. Novit enim Dominus qui sunt eius"—"Kill them all. God will recognize his own"—originating a slogan that seven hundred years later would be silk-screened on T-shirts you could buy at the county fair, usually with a skull in a black beret nearby. In the same bins, you could find shirts illustrated with a picture of a naked and seemingly headless man, though his head, on closer inspection, was wedged between his buttocks. The caption said, "Your problem is obvious." Wilfredo was the right age to appreciate these shirts, but the last time we took him to our county fair, he was only interested in the stuffed animals they were giving as prizes at the sharpshooting booth.) There's no telling how many cats were killed during this period— enough, according to some commentators, that in parts of Europe their numbers were greatly suppressed. In the absence of their natural predator, rats flourished, and when the Black Death arrived in 1347, inundating Christendom with sweat, pus, and black blood, it may in part have been because there were so many rats around to spread it. Some 100 million people died wretchedly. Novit enim Dominus qui sunt eius.

A footnote: before it decided to exterminate the Cathars, the church tried to convert them. It delegated the task to one Diego de Guzman, whom it later canonized as St. Dominic. The order he founded, the Dominicans, became known as the "dogs of God" (*domini* + *cani*) for the enthusiasm with which its members sniffed out heresy. Once they'd wiped out the Cathars, they shifted their operations to Protestants and crypto-Jews.

On the night Bitey dislocated F.'s arm, I sat beside her on one of the emergency room's brittle bucket seats, filling out the admissions forms for her because she couldn't use her right hand. How pale she was in that diagnostic light! I could see every vein in her eyelids. I had to keep asking her questions; I didn't know her medical history, let alone her insurance provider, and shock made her vague and slow to anwer. I could remember snapping at my mother in similar circumstances as a teenager ("What do you mean you don't know what medicines you're taking?") and was relieved I'd become at least a little more patient since then. Maybe it was because I knew that on some level the accident was my fault. In Texas, your neighbors can sue you if you let your cattle stray onto their land, and I imagine the damages are higher if somebody dislocates an arm because of it.

Much of the anger I used to feel back when I was checking my mother into the hospital (for pleurisy, for pneumonia, for hepatitis, for herniated disks, for a spot on the lung that might be cancer but wasn't, though twenty-odd years later it would be) had been anger at being attached to her, yoked to her, *with her*, the last being the way you identify yourself as a teenager. At least I did when I was one.

"Are you with her?" pronounced "*huh.*"

"No, man, I'm not with *huh*. I'm with Fran."

"He's with Carol and those Walden kids."

"She's with those heads who hang out by the fountain." That need to place yourself in a context, with a girlfriend or boyfriend, ideally, but failing that with a group or clique or, that word of wincing recollection, a *tribe*. Our egos were still unfinished—in places they were only dotted lines—and so we needed to borrow parts of each other's. But after spending an afternoon and evening, sometimes even a whole weekend, hanging out with my tribe, smoking hash and snorting crushed-up Dexamyl with the children of shrinks and advertising executives in an apartment overlooking Central Park, I went home to the apartment where I lived with my mother, and then I was with *huh*. In the hospital, it was worse. Our affiliation would be evident to anyone who might be passing through the waiting room. One of the few questions I didn't have to ask her was the names of her emergency contacts: the first was my grandfather; the second was me.

And now I was with F. I was happy to be with her, even proud, though, really, what else could I have done: waved bye-bye as the EMTs slid her into their ambulance, then gone inside to make myself a late-night sandwich? I felt a small pang of disappointment when for emergency contact, she asked me to put down her mother. It wasn't until we got married two years later that she started putting me down instead. From a logical standpoint, there's no reason why I should have cared so much, beyond being the first, rather than the second, person to learn that something bad had happened to her or having the privilege of bringing F.'s medications and makeup to her in the hospital, along with the boxy terrycloth robe she likes to wear, the one with a picture of a sitting cat on the back. Still, it mattered to me. I wanted my name on her forms.

About a year before this, F. had taken *me* to the hospital. I'd developed a persistent headache, and although I've had so many headaches in the course of my life that I've become a connoisseur of them, the way people are of cheeses, this was a kind I'd never had before. It was localized on the right side of my head, and the pain seemed to originate in a spot on the surface, as if I'd been rapped there with a hammer. It hurt for days; Advil did nothing for it. And one night, as we were leaving a movie, F. asked me what was wrong, and I said wonderingly, "It's still there," and she asked me if I wanted to go to the hospital. I said no. Then I said maybe. Then we were in the emergency room of St. Vincent's. Ten years before, this had been the charnel house of New York. Every day, dozens came here to die, not all at once but a few lurching steps at a time. They had boiling fevers, faces mottled with cancer, diseases that before this had been seen only in birds. The doctors hauled them back, stabilized them, and sent them home, but a few weeks later they returned, sicker. After a while, they died.

By the time I finally saw a doctor, I was starting to doubt that I was in as much pain as I'd thought I was. I was also bored and embarrassed at having dragged my girlfriend to a hospital on a Saturday night instead of a nice restaurant. We were in a yawning chamber sectioned like an orange by flimsy curtains, through which we glimpsed dim shapes of suffering humans attended by other humans dressed in white, green, and powder blue. My doctor was a young Israeli woman with lovely breasts that proclaimed their splendor beneath her open lab coat. It was all I could do not to stare at them as she bent over me. Later F. told me how funny I'd looked, following the beam of my caregiver's pencil light until my gaze intersected her boobs, at which point it froze raptly and then swerved. Maybe the doctor saw this too. I remember thinking she looked very amused considering she was examining somebody who might be having an aneurism.

She left for a while, cautioning me not to move too much. Throughout the examination, I'd been distantly aware of a continual sound, soft, feeble, monotonous as the hiss of a respirator. Only now did I recognize it as moaning. It was coming from the examining area to our right. The voice was a man's. "Help me, doctor," it kept saying. "It hurts, it hurts bad." It was awful, the awfulness coming from the voice's mechanical character and from the rupture between the mechanical and the human—the animal—truth of pain. Every animal understands pain, but as far as I know, no one has yet built a machine that does. "What's wrong with that guy?" I asked F. Because she was sitting rather than lying down, she could see him. "I don't know, he looks like he might be mentally ill." The moment she said it, I knew she was right. "Help me, doctor," the voice said again. F. and I looked at each other.

I don't remember either of us saying anything—maybe we squeezed hands—but we both turned our attention to the droning sufferer behind the curtain. We—how do I put this?— we willed him better. No, we understood that our wills weren't that powerful. We sent him kindly thoughts. My kindly thought was, "You're okay, friend, you're okay." I don't know exactly what F.'s was. When I think back to that night, I'm not sure how I knew we were thinking the same thing at the same time. Maybe I didn't know in the moment and just extrapolated from what she told me later. That's one of the epistemological problems of a long relationship. You're never sure what you actually know and what you reconstruct from your partner's reports after the fact. I'm not crazy about the word "partner"; it suggests the work of marriage but not the pleasure. But it's true that people in a relationship are partners in recording its history, like two scholars who join efforts to write a chronicle of a small, unimportant town where something out of the ordinary once happened. In a successful relationship, the partners' accounts more or less tally. They may differ in detail, but the overall narrative is consistent, and so is the tone. But then there are histories where nothing matches, so that in adjoining sentences the townspeople are good Catholics and devout Cathars, living harmoniously and in gnashing enmity. *But we used to be so happy. I was never happy. Never.*

On the other side of the curtain, the voice underwent a change. It still sounded mechanical, but the machine was slowing. In time it would stop. It said, "Thank you, doctor.

Thank you." Disregarding instructions, I sat up and peered through the curtain. Silhouetted behind it I saw a slouching, shirtless man with a soft, matronly stomach. F. and I grinned at each other. A moment later we started laughing. Laughing worsened the pain in my head, but it seemed worth it.

A while afterward, the Israeli doctor came back and told me that what I had was a stress headache. "It's very common," she reassured me. "Especially in men your age." Mildly, I reminded her that I'd never had a headache like this before. It was bad enough having a doctor with breasts see me as middle-aged; I didn't want her seeing me as middle-aged and hypochondriacal. She shrugged. "Maybe you never had stress before."

Cats are supposed to be solitary creatures, but when you live with multiples of them, you become aware of their social interactions. These are less boisterous than those of dogs, which usually involve running and panting, tails wagging and tongues flying like flags. What goes on among cats is more complex and mercurial, with small, unexpected shifts of power and moments when hostility abruptly gives way to solidarity, or vice versa. At mealtimes, each is conscious of what the others are getting. Biscuit would often look up from her bowl to glance at the cat nearest her, then give it a cuff—not a hard cuff but hard enough to make it back away—at which point she'd move over and help herself to its shreds or pellets or, my favorite stroke of the marketing people at Friskies, "classic paté," which appeals at the same time to snobbery and squeamishness. She didn't seem to mind if the loser changed places with her. She might have forgotten that the protein it was eating had once been hers. Or maybe she didn't care; it was just sloppy seconds. Considering the feline reputation for independence, their values are surprisingly conformist: a cat wants what other cats want. It wants it because they want it. It wants other cats to want what it has. F. once gave Suki a piece of cheese and noticed that instead of polishing it off right away, the crabby gray tabby held it between her paws until she saw Tina enter the room. Only then did she begin eating her prize in tearing mouthfuls, pausing from time to time to look intently at the other cat.

The gaze is important to them; they want to see and be seen. Biscuit was drawn to houses that had cats living in them and showed a preference for ones where the cats were kept indoors. There was one where she'd loiter for hours, clambering onto one of the downstairs windows (she was never a very good jumper) so she could peer inside and, I'm pretty sure, display herself to the inmates. Sitting broadside on the sill, she'd lick her paws in a way that put me in mind of someone buffing her nails. Behold, she might have been saying, here is a free creature who goes where she pleases and helps herself to the bounty of lawn and hedgerow!

They want you to look at them, too, but not too long, since that might indicate you're thinking of eating them. I no longer remember who first taught me that if you blink slowly at a cat two or three times, the cat will blink back, the same as it would at another of its kind. You're supposedly assuring it that you mean it no harm. Of course, I'd observed this for years among friends' cats without knowing its significance. It was just an example of their minimal style of relating. Once I learned what blinking meant, I couldn't resist practicing it with Bitey. I must have spent hours blinking at her as we sat across from each other in my living room in Baltimore or, later, in apartments in New York, the sounds of the river of worldly glamor lapping through the windows. I'd look at her from the sofa. There she sat with her forepaws together and her tail coiled around them, her chin slightly tucked. I blinked and waited, blinked again. I was listening to Marvin Gaye or Robyn Hitchcock, love raw as the mark of an axe in a half-felled tree or sheathed in irony, though, really, what's so ironic about "I feel beautiful because you love me," except maybe the marimbas? Again I blinked. Bitey blinked back. It never ceased to make me happy.

Although cats are the most popular pet in the United States, there are way more dog books than cat books—not just guides to their care and training but narratives, both fictional and true. Stories of heroic dogs, mischievous dogs, incorrigible dogs, loyal dogs, loveable dogs, life-transforming dogs. It's easier to write about a dog than a cat. With dogs, there's always something going on. They race to greet you at the door; they jump up and plant their paws on your chest; they muzzle your crotch; they bring you things they want you to throw to them or to try to pull from their mouths. They bark at you: all you have to do is say, "Speak!" They look at you with eyes brimming with meaning, and the wonderful thing about that meaning is you don't have to interpret it; it's obvious. Maybe it's the thousands of years they spent hunting beside us, learning to read us, learning to make themselves readable. A dog is a dictionary without definitions, just words that mean nothing but themselves. Feed me! Play with me! Walk me! Love me! The object of these sentences is "me," but their unvoiced subject is always "you." Whose knee are they pawing if not yours? At whose feet have they dropped that frisbee, tooth-marked and sopping? Into whose eyes are they gazing? With dogs, it's all about you. No wonder they're easy to write about.

A cat may look at you, too, it's true, but it will look just as fixedly at a wall. No other creature displays such free-floating intentness. How to distinguish between the gaze that says something and the gaze that says nothing at all? If nobody had ever told me what a cat's blinking means, would I have figured it out on my own? The pleasure of dog ownership is having an animal that speaks your language, or a language that shares many terms with yours, like Swedish and Norwegian. A cat doesn't speak your language. But when I blinked at Bitey and she blinked back, I briefly had the illusion that I could speak hers.

~~~

The South Carolina border was marked by signs for a nearby fireworks emporium. Fireworks were legal in South Carolina, along with every type of firearm, including AK-47s and twelve-gauge tactical personal-defense shotguns designed for the homeowner who needed to drive off a bloodthirsty mob. Folks in North Carolina didn't know what they were missing. They might, though, if they lived close enough to the state line. The signs were that big. As I approached, I had another moment of temptation in which I wondered how many cherry bombs I could get for twenty bucks and whether they'd let me take them on the plane as long as I checked my bag. The temptation passed quickly. It wasn't that strong to begin with. Given a choice between fireworks and a lap dance, I'd rather have a lap dance. I stopped at a light and, looking up, saw the head of an immense black cat snarling at me from the roadside with a mouth wide as the gate of hell. Its nose and tongue glowed as if red hot.

My God, who would want that as a pet?

~ ~ ~

F. had men before she met me, some of whom she saw for a year or more, some of whom she loved. But she's spent most of her adult life alone. I think I have never met anyone more lonely. Her solitude, along with her quiet and general eccentricity, has caused her social awkwardness. For a long time she didn't drive, and she didn't own a car until we bought one together; even in the country, she got around by walking and, because of that, was viewed with pity, condescension, and occasional unease. She was an affront to people's sense of categories. Walking was an activity of the poor and the health-conscious elderly, and F. was youthful and well dressed. Sales clerks don't know what to do with her. She doesn't get small talk and when strangers try to make it with her, she looks at them with a clinical bafflement that's easy to mistake for disdain. One of the first things she told me about herself was that she was often insulted at parties. At first I doubted her—why would anybody do that?—but as I started going to parties with her, I saw that it was true. Maybe it wasn't actual insults, but people slighted her, seemingly for no reason. She assured me it happened less when I was with her. It was one of the things she liked about being together.

It's true that I'm more socially adroit than she is, more comfortable with the insincerities that ease open the stubborn cupboard drawers of small-town life. The Friday evenings at the restaurant whose bartender used to rake leaves off your front lawn when he was a little kid. The New Year's Eve party held in the dreary strip mall near the entrance to the highway—not even a strip mall but a cluster of unfrequented small businesses anchored by a diner that's had four or five different managements in the time you've lived here—one of whose storefronts now turns out to contain a dance club. Who knew, a dance club barely a quarter of a mile from the fencing-and-gazebo barn? In the semidarkness, middle-aged revelers perform the jogging steps of the middle-aged alongside teenage girls in shiny, skimpy dresses and their boyfriends. A bass grunts. Some people are wearing domino masks, which conjures up an image of the orgy in *Eyes Wide Shut*. And like that movie's protagonist, who sees the familiar skin of the world peeled back to reveal its secret sensual anatomy, you realize that these partygoers are people you know. The man in the snappy black-and-white tuxedo shirt lifts weights beside you at the gym. The woman in the sequined pantsuit owns the dry cleaner's. Her husband always calls you by F.'s last name. What you're supposed to do is give the bartender a good tip and ask him how his mom is. You're supposed to tease the orgiast from the gym: "So *this* is why you been doing all those flies? You wanted to look good for your New Year's date?" F. wouldn't do that; it wouldn't occur to her to.

After we got married, my actual presence at such events became less necessary, since she now wore a wedding band. "People notice that," she'd say, flashing the ring, "and I can see the relief on their faces. They know how to place me." She still says it, even now that what we are to each other is uncertain. There are women who find a wedding band demeaning, since it essentially serves as an emblem of possession, a function that was more evident when only women wore them. The ring signifies that the wearer belongs to a certain man and can't be taken from him without consequence. In that sense, it's also a warning device, like a car alarm. It's unclear whether the warning is directed at other men or at the woman herself. But, along the same demeaning lines, you could also compare a wedding band to a pet's ID tag; typically, dogs get a bone-shaped one and cats a silent little bell. Such tags also express ownership and, indeed, often proclaim it, being engraved with the name and phone number of the pet's owner. But their purpose isn't to prevent theft so much as to help find the pet if it gets lost. Pets get lost all the time. Drawn by an interesting smell—in cartoons it's typically portrayed as a vaporous hand with a beckoning finger — they slip their leash or wander out of their yard and soon find themselves on a street they don't recognize, gazing up at the legs of oblivious hurrying strangers. Sometimes they roam farther still, beyond the places where people are. A landscape of rustling underbrush and yellow eyes glinting in the shadows of the trees. A dark wood in which there is no straight path.

There's no archaeological record of when men and women began to marry. Given that some form of marriage exists among nomadic peoples like the Tuareg, Kham, and Warrungu, it's likely that humans were marrying before they had much in the way of property. So much for Engels's view of marriage as a bourgeois institution. Say in the beginning its chief purpose was the protection and rearing of small children and the formation of alliances among people who might otherwise be enemies. That rangy fellow with the dead eye and the necklace of dog's teeth wasn't so menacing when you discovered he was the husband of your wife's sister, and you were grateful to be able to call on him when other nomads tried to drive you away from the watering hole. Marriage extended kinship beyond biology, connected you to people who didn't share your blood. In all the early accounts of marriage, the idea of connection is paramount. When God gives Adam a mate, it's not in the interest of his sexual fulfillment. It's because it is not good that the man should be alone.

This period of companionship lasted only a little while. Perhaps it ended with the Fall. Having seen each other turned inside out like flayed skins, could the man and the woman stand to look at each other again? Could they stand to be looked at? In Masaccio's painting, they walk side by side but don't touch. Both of them are encysted in their shame, and one wouldn't be surprised to learn that once they had wandered a distance out of Eden and begotten their unhappy sons, they parted ways and had nothing more to do with each other. It established a pattern. Men labored with men and went off to war with them; they feasted and got drunk together and sang the kinds of songs men have been singing since they discovered that they sounded better when they were drinking. The women served them, first the food, then the bowls of wine or beer. There was no pretense of fairness. Afterward, they went off by themselves and ate and drank the women's portion and sang songs of their own. At a certain hour of the night, the men and women lay down together. Things went on in this manner, with variations, for the next 10,000 years.

Societies that observe this arrangement are described as homosocial, with men and women inhabiting separate spheres that only narrowly coincide.

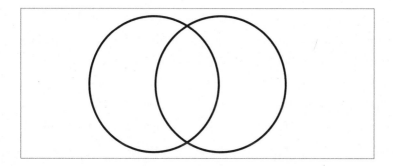

In some times and places, the sexes dined together.

Michelangelo Merisi da Caravaggio, *Salome with the Head of John the Baptist* (London, c. 1607), National Gallery, London. Courtesy of Art Resource.

Sometimes they came together for worship or to attend public entertainments.

But for much of history, the chief area of coincidence was marriage, especially the marriage ceremony, in which a man and woman stood together before their families, under the eye of that God who decreed it wasn't good for man to be alone. From then on, they were one, or at least they were treated as one by their society, that one being, implicitly, male. The paradox was that once the man and the woman had publicly sealed their union, they largely returned to their separate social realms. One can visualize marriage as a smaller version of the compound giant pictured on the original frontispiece of Hobbes's *Leviathan*.

Abraham Bosse, frontispiece of the first edition of Thomas Hobbes's *Leviathan* (1651). Courtesy of the Granger Collection.

Instead of being made up of thousands of men, the leviathan of marriage contains a single man and woman. The face it wears in public is a male face; it resembles the husband's face, but it has just one unvarying expression, sober, contented, a little dull. The leviathan appears in public only on rare, mostly ceremonial occasions. The rest of the time, it breaks up into its constituent male and female homunculi, and these spend much of their time with others of their kind. Or this was the practice until well into the last century.

However, even when engaged in her own pursuits, the woman is now identified as belonging to—as being of—the leviathan or, for all practical purposes, her husband. It's as if instead of wearing a ring, she were carrying a little mask (I imagine it as being made of gold) with her husband's face on it, and on certain occasions she must hold the face in front of hers and speak from behind it, as if in keeping with Genesis 20:16: "Behold, he is to thee a covering of the eyes." Depending on the husband's status, this can be advantageous. Witness the courtesies accorded the wives of the baron, the mayor, and the pastor in former times, the wives of celebrities and corporate CEOs today. The prie-dieu embroidered with the family coronet. The personal shopping assistant at Barney's. Of course, it's oppressive for a woman to have to go through the world pretending to be her husband, but the masquerade doesn't just carry privilege: it carries protection. In a man's world, an unmarried woman is up for grabs. She may be raped. She may be robbed. She may be tortured and murdered, even burned alive before crowds that one variously imagines as raucous or dumbstruck by the spectacle of suffering unfolding before them. This was what was done to witches. (Some witches, of course, were married women. In a man's world, finally, any woman is up for grabs, and a husband's protection is about the same as that provided by a fig leaf.)

~~~

There were no great witch hunts in Europe until late in the fourteenth century. During what is called the Dark Ages, the church denounced the belief in witchcraft as superstition, and in AD 794 the Council of Frankfurt made the burning of witches punishable by death. I wonder whether the resurgence of the practice owed anything to the extinction of the Cathar heresy a hundred years before. I don't mean a Halliburton-like conspiracy on the part of the Inquisition, which, having done away with the Cathars, needed another threat to justify its continued operations. By 1480, it already had Protestants for that. But people like to believe in the hidden enemy, the worm in the fruit. Protestants weren't hidden; they nailed proclamations to cathedral doors. The Cathars were hidden, at least some of the time. And what could be more hidden than the woman who lives in your village, maybe even next door to you, distinguished from her sisters only by the fact that she is alone, with no man to vouch for her? For company, she may keep an animal, which is actually a disguised demon. At their esbats or sabbats, witches were said to fornicate with goats, but in the popular imagination, as enshrined in the Halloween displays at Target and CVS, the witch's familiar is usually a cat, a black one.

I think back to the way cats clean their dirty parts, I mean, hunching forward while holding a leg up in the air, presumably to give them fuller access to the area in need of cleaning. What distinguished Biscuit's approach to hygiene, as I said, is the combination of precision and abandon, the geometric line of the suspended leg and the shapeless slouch of the rest of her, which created the impression — at least it did in me — of a creature burrowing into herself as if trying to disappear, so intent on disappearing that she'd forgotten about one part of herself, her raised hind leg. And it's this hind leg that I imagine remaining poised in the air after the rest of Biscuit made her impossible exit, like the needle of an invisible compass quivering toward an invisible north.

Of course, Biscuit wouldn't be the first cat to vanish and leave a part of itself behind. Lewis Carroll's grinning Cheshire

Sir John Tenniel, "The Cheshire Cat," illustration from the first edition of Lewis Carroll's *Alice's Adventures in Wonderland* (1865). Courtesy of the Granger Collection.

Cat vanishes repeatedly, at first with such abruptness that Alice complains it makes her dizzy.

"'All right,' said the Cat, and this time," Carroll tells us, "it vanished quite slowly, beginning with the end of the tail, and ending with the grin, which remained some time after the rest of it had gone."

Carroll may have been inspired by a Cheshire cheese that was made in a mold shaped like a smiling cat. The cheese was cut from the tail end, which would make the grinning head the last part to be eaten. But it's also true that beings seldom vanish all at once. Mostly they do it slowly, almost imperceptibly, until one day you look at the space they occupied and see it's empty. Or almost empty, since it's also the case that most beings leave some trace of themselves behind. A smile lingering above the branch of a tree. The scent on a blouse. A leg pointing at nothing.

We went to events in the city, of course, especially in our early years together, when I still had the loft, and these were more comfortable for F. because she knew most of the people at them. Some of them were her friends, and others were fellow travelers in the worlds she moved through, the worlds of readings and art openings and awards dinners where the small, exquisite portions usually went half eaten, not because the food was bad but because people were too excited or too anxious or worried about spilling something on the Armani or being photographed with their mouths gaping to admit a forkful of some other thing, I don't know what, duck confit. I used to take great pleasure in imitating what someone might look like in such a photo, my head tilted to one side, my eyes popping with greed, my teeth—which were still very bad back then, back before the dental work I'll be paying off for the rest of my life—bared. It always made F. laugh. In fairness to her, she may have been the first of us to do the imitation.

F. didn't like all the people she knew at these events; really, she disliked many of them, much more than I did. Well, she knew them. And she understood what drove them, the slow- or quick-fused ambition, the desire for money or fame or beauty and glamour, beauty and glamour especially, always paired, as if one couldn't exist without the other. F. also wanted those things. "If only I had legs like hers," she'd sigh, gazing with forlorn admiration at a woman across the room. "My whole life would've been different." But she made no effort to disguise her appetite; she'd tell a stranger about it. She hated the people who pretended to have no appetite and viewed any display of hunger with pitying amusement, even as they peered over your shoulder to see what you had on your plate.

To me, beauty and glamour seemed so unattainable that I could only respond to them with cowed sullenness. F. sensed my discomfort long before I told her about it, which in the beginning I couldn't, and for a long time she'd stay close to me when we went to events where beauty and glamour were likely to be present. The way she did it didn't feel protective so much as proprietary. I was hers, and she wanted to be seen with me. I was always grateful for this. I liked it even better if she went off to talk with somebody she knew for a while, leaving me free to wander around the room or stand in a corner, hoping that I looked mysterious rather than just awkward as I surveyed the space's other occupants. Few of them, to be honest, were truly beautiful or glamorous, except for the occasional fashion model slipping past like a gazelle that had been imported into a barnyard in the mistaken belief that it could be mated with the livestock. I guess what I liked about F.'s absences was the evidence that she trusted me not to fall apart or try to mount one of the gazelles or get in a fight with a strange bull while she was gone. And I loved to watch her making her way back across the room toward me. When she spotted me, I could see the questing look in her eyes give way to pleasure; I was what she'd been looking for. Sometimes, though, she'd manage to sneak up behind me and grab me around the waist. She's proud of her stealth, and she got a kick out of the little start I gave, though the truth is I often started on purpose.

"Behold, he is to thee a covering of the eyes." The speaker is King Abimelech of Gerar. He's addressing Sarah, the wife of Abraham. Many commentators believe he's scolding her, though, really, if he should be scolding anybody, it's Abraham, who passed off Sarah as his sister, under which misimpression Abimelech "took her" (Gen. 20:2) as his wife. "Took": the word is, to put it mildly, vexing. The Hebrew *laqach* is defined as "to take (in the widest applications)," which could include rape or the sort of nuptial kidnapping that was still being practiced symbolically by the lusty groomsmen of France at the close of the Middle Ages. This is one of two times in Genesis that Abraham pretends he and Sarah aren't married. On both occasions, he's afraid that some powerful figure—before Abimelech, it was the pharaoh of Egypt—will covet his ninety-year-old wife and have him killed in order to possess her. The subterfuge saves his skin, but at the cost of her chastity, or the near cost, depending on how you read "took." Abimelech insists he never laid a finger on Sarah. Or, at least, that's what he says when God appears to him in a dream and tells him he's a dead man for taking liberties with her, and even if he's lying, you can hardly blame him. I mean, who knew?

Most biblical commentaries put forth the view that "a covering of the eyes" refers to the veil that was worn by married women in the ancient Middle East and is still worn there today, and not just by married women. The phrase is syntactically ambiguous. Whose eyes are being covered, the veiled woman's or the lustful viewer's? In either case, the purpose of the veil is the same, and when Abimelech tells Sarah, "He is to thee a covering of the eyes," he's defining a husband's responsibility to his wife: to be her veil, the protector of her modesty. Not because that modesty is important to him (it doesn't seem to be important to Abraham), but because it may matter to her. That the patriarchy values something doesn't mean that women may not value it too, for reasons that have nothing to do with men's claims on their bodies. Masaccio's Eve shields her breasts and sex without any prompting from Adam, who, locked behind the visor of his grief, may not even notice that she's naked. The patriarchs are often held up as models of marital conduct—this is especially so in fundamentalist Christian circles—but Adam seems awfully wishy-washy, and Abraham is even worse. The slights and betrayals. The fling with his wife's handmaid, who flashes her pregnant belly like a big piece of bling—*Look what your husband gave me*—until the wife gets fed up and makes him cast her out into the desert, and the kid with her. The spineless way he hands Sarah off to any big shot who looks at her twice. Jews aren't supposed to do that. Eskimos are supposed to do that.

We think of modesty mostly in sexual terms, as a reaction — even an anticipatory reaction — to sexual excitement, an attempt to rein in its lunging surge. Eve covers her sexual parts, not her face. That Adam covers his face might support Freud's belief that women are intrinsically more modest than men, but it also suggests that modesty can be construed more broadly. There is a modesty of the body and a modesty of the soul. Both can be outraged. And there is a social modesty that deters some people from calling attention to where they come from or who their parents were or how much money they have and causes other people to lie about those things; in the latter case, one speaks not of modesty but of shame. Beyond shielding his wife from the gaze and touch of other men, the husband's task may be to help her navigate in social space, for it's there that she is most likely to be shamed. The social realm is where shame lives.

Once, early on in our marriage, I met F. for dinner at a restaurant with our friend Scott. I was late, and when I got there, they were already eating and a second man was sitting across from Scott, in the seat next to mine. I knew him, but not to speak to. He was an old guy who had once done something on Broadway; it made him one of our town's celebrities. Arthur had a wide, loose-lipped mouth framed by the ponderous jowls of a cartoon bulldog. You could imagine them wobbling in outrage or exertion or, less often, from laughter. I had a sense

of him as someone who was used to watching impassively as
other people laughed at his jokes but would under no circumstances laugh at anybody else's. Laughter was tribute, and he
refused to pay it. Sitting diagonally across from him, F. looked
particularly delicate, an impression heightened by the way she
cut her food into small, precise bites that she placed in her
mouth one by one with small flourishes of her fork while she
held up the other hand before her like a paw. I don't know why
she eats this way, but to me it's part of her charm.

I remember the drift of the conversation. F. was talking
about her appetite, which is robust for somebody her size and
used to be even more so. When she was younger, she likes to
brag, she could put away a plate of fries and follow it with a
milkshake and a piece of pie and never put on a pound.
Maybe that's what she said that evening. "That doesn't surprise me," Arthur said. It sounded like the windup to a joke,
but in the next moment, his voice darkened. "I don't doubt
you'd eat anything." The darkness was the darkness of con-
tempt, of loathing. F. stared at him. Somebody else might
have said, "Excuse me?" which would have given Arthur the
opening to pretend he'd been joking. But F.'s quicker than
that, and what she said back was quick and biting. It may have
been, "I guess you'd know"; that would have been appropri-
ate. She didn't raise her voice, but her anger was unmistak-
able. Looking back, I think Arthur had counted on her to be
too startled to defend herself. Maybe he was drunk; he had a
reputation as a drunk. He told F., "I can just imagine the
kinds of garbage you put in your mouth."

Inanely, I turned to look at him. He was leaning back in his chair. His jowls were inflamed. He might have been resting after a bout of gluttony. Scott called for the check. We tossed down bills and credit cards as if our money had become hateful to us and avoided each other's eyes while we waited for our change. Arthur heaved himself back from the table and made for the men's room. "Who is that pig?" F. asked me. Her eyes were bright with hatred. "Why didn't you say something?"

If I reconstruct the incident, which probably lasted no more than three minutes from start to finish, less than a short pop song in the days of AM radio, it took me several seconds to realize that the loathsome old hack had been insulting F. The rest of the time, I'd been floundering for a response. If Arthur had been younger, I might just have said, "Watch it, buddy!" which isn't clever but gets a point across, but he was old, and I was raised to defer to old people. I said none of this to F. I knew better than to excuse myself. I only said I was sorry and for months afterward imagined an alternate version of the evening in which I grabbed Arthur's wine glass and flung its contents in his face.

I got my revenge a few years later, at another restaurant, where I was eating with Scott and his girlfriend. Arthur came up to our table on his way out. In the moment I saw him, my face was suffused with a terrible heat, not the heat of a blush but the heat that assails you when you open the door of a furnace. I half believed you could see it burning across the room. But Arthur seemed not to notice. He spoke with my friends, then turned to me with an outstretched hand. He'd lost weight since I'd last seen him, and this, together with a certain vagueness to his gaze, created an impression of diminishment. I looked at him steadily but kept my hand at my side. Then I looked away. It might have been satisfying if I hadn't heard that in the time since that wretched dinner he'd had a stroke. He may not have recognized me; he may not have remembered insulting F. That whole portion of his memory may have been torn from his mind like a sheet of paper from a notebook and crumpled into a ball and tossed, coincidentally, into the garbage, which, in any event, is what it had become.

F.'s recollection of the original fight—or say the ambush, since neither she nor I could be said to have fought back—is different from mine. After we parted ways with Scott and got into the car, she says I turned to her and snapped, "I really didn't appreciate you embarrassing me in front of my friend."

~~~

During the hour-and-a-half drive from the college town to the airport, I passed through the following localities:

Belville
Bolivia
Supply
Shallotte (pronounced *Shal*-lot)
Carolina Shores, skipping a side trip to nearby Calabash
Little River
Myrtle Beach

If I hadn't been in a hurry, I might've stopped in Wampee.

On reflection, my explanation for why I waited till October 2 feels like bullshit to me. I have to wonder whether the sleepless nights, the hysterical phone calls and e-mails (by now I'd deputed at least two of my friends to come by the house and call my cat at different times), weren't just a front, a lot of thrashing, hand-wringing activity thrown up to disguise a vacuum. Maybe I was just lazy. Maybe I didn't love my cat, or didn't love her as much as I thought. I mean, it's hard enough to know when you love a person.

~ ~ ~

In one of his later lectures, Jacques Derrida poses the question of why, if he walks naked into the bathroom and his cat follows him inside and looks at him, as a cat will, he feels ashamed. Derrida sees this shame as a measure of the boundary, which is to some extent an arbitrary one, drawn up by bribed surveyors, between the human and the animal. He connects his shame to the shame our ancestors felt when they ate the forbidden fruit and realized for the first time that they were naked. In this scenario, Derrida's cat may stand in for God; its gaze stands in for the Creator's gaze, being similarly unblinking and inscrutable. Really, all Western representations of God are deficient inasmuch as they give God the eyes of a human being rather than those of a cat.

Is nakedness a condition unique to humans? Is naked something only a human can be? In French, a synonym for naked is *à poil*, "down to the hair," the hair being that of a beast. A naked human, then, is a human stripped down to a bestial state, in which it is cold and fearful and ashamed. In contrast, an animal that has its hair has everything it needs, and most attempts at improving its condition only cause it discomfort. Witness the evident discomfort of a cat dressed in human clothing.

The cat pictured above might be called an image of offended modesty.

Right after the man and woman ate the fruit of the Tree of Knowledge, they began acting strangely, and the dog and cat in the garden watched them with perplexity. They were the same creatures they had been a moment before, mangy, sparse coated, moving clumsily about on their hind legs. But something about them was different. They shivered and cast anxious looks about them. They drew together but shrank from each other's touch. Strangest of all, they plucked leaves from the tree and tried to cover themselves with them. Why were they doing that? Today we have forgotten the moment when our forebears first knew they were naked and were ashamed. But the cat and the dog remember, and that is why they look at us so intently, wondering what changed us.

6

Just past Little River, I had to take a turnoff onto Route 9 and then merge onto Highway 31 South toward Myrtle Beach. The sign for the turnoff was smaller than the ones I was used to up north; I could easily have missed it. The ramp jogged gently—to my mind, sneakily—to the right, then swung back and climbed so that I found myself arcing over the continuation of the road I had just been on and an unpicturesque wetland where dead-looking trees rose out of brown water. No wonder the bastards were so mad to develop here. Who wanted to see that shit on the way to the beach? The traffic I'd been congratulating myself on missing was suddenly thick about me, blades of late sun glancing off its hoods and grilles. How clean those cars were.

A few years before I'd been in a town in Florida where people drove their pickups on the beach, not twenty feet from the breaking surf, truck after truck in a slow, martial procession whose brutish throat-clearing drowned out the sound of waves.

I was working with a famous monologist who was in the middle of a breakdown. A bunch of us had taken him to the beach as therapy, but when he got out of the car and saw those trucks, he staggered back in fear. A moment later he glanced upward and dropped into a crouch, shielding his face with his hands. He choked out a cry. "Shark!" And following his gaze, I saw that there really was a shark overhead, a great, swooping shark-shaped kite whose grinning mouth stretched to devour the world, and us with it. Two years later, the monologist killed himself by jumping off a ferryboat into the freezing water of New York Harbor.

Now, caught in traffic on an overpass above another beach, I thought about poor Biscuit. I worried that she must be afraid in her exile, far from home, assailed by strange sounds and smells: the trembling hoot of night owls, the bloodthirsty mirth of coyotes closing in on their prey, the acrid scat of animals that feed on other animals. At the time, I thought nothing could be more terrible than such fear. Only looking back do I understand that whatever Biscuit encountered in the wild, it would be something that on some level she already knew, that she recognized by instinct. The wild was where she'd been born, after all, or at least found, and she'd had no way of knowing that the dogs baying up at her were people's house pets. Nothing she encountered in the woods near our home would be as strange to her as the sight of trucks driving along the edge of the ocean or a Mylar shark wheeling and flapping in the sky. She might fear for her life, but she wouldn't fear she was going mad. I doubt a cat has even the remotest sense of what that might mean. And I can't imagine the circumstances under which Biscuit would dive into an endless expanse of dull gray water, water cold enough to stop the heart, wanting it to be stopped. Only a human would do that.

~~~

On those mornings when I came into the bathroom naked and Biscuit looked up at me from the radiator, where she'd settled sometime after slipping off the bed during the night, I don't think that what I felt was shame. I don't think I was even especially conscious of being naked. I might *become* conscious of it on those occasions when I petted my cat, which she seemed to have invited me to do by rolling over and stretching, displaying her luxuriously soft (and, because of where she'd been lying, luxuriously warm) stomach, and she seized my hand and began to lick it while lightly raking it with her extended claws. (I'm pretty sure she wasn't doing this to hurt me but to keep my hand from getting away.) At that moment I'd be suddenly aware of the temptation my genitals might present to a creature programmed by instinct to strike at dangling objects, and I'd retract my groin as far as I could while letting her go on grooming my unresisting hand. To me, this is not shame; it's awareness of my vulnerability, though maybe what I'm really talking about is fear. Maybe when Derrida speaks of shame he really means fear. Maybe he was ashamed to admit he was afraid of his cat.

What might Biscuit have made of my nakedness? She must have recognized it as being different from the state in which she usually saw me, covered in soft, warm fabrics that were so pleasant to sit on—she especially sought out my lap when I was wearing my flannel bathrobe—and that bore my scent along with the odors of coffee, garlic and olive oil, tea tree oil chewing sticks, motor oil and grass cuttings, laundry detergent, and household cleaners. She knew most of those smells from the house and its environs, and when she detected them on me, she must have had an idea of where I'd been and what I'd been doing: preparing the bitter black water I drank every morning, with a shameful waste of the rich, sweet milk that ought to go in her dish; pushing the growling thing that chewed up the grass in strips; going out to fetch the paper bags from which I took the things F. and I ate and then left out for her to climb into so that no one could see her. Sometimes I'd come into the house smelling of things that had no counterpart in her experience: the subway, on days I'd been working in the city. What would she make of that, a canned stew of humans shrieking through the darkness beneath the earth? Some other cat might think it was a kind of pound, a pound for humans. But Biscuit had never been in a pound.

And what went on in her mind when she watched me undress, before I took a shower, for instance? To undress is to cross the threshold from clothed to naked, and judging by the intentness with which she studied me, the procedure interested her. Did she see my discarded clothing as a foreign layer that I'd managed to slough off, as she might manage to disentangle herself from one of the shopping bags she nested in? Or did she see it as part of me, like a skin or, really, like fur, which was part of her but could also be shed: if only it weren't shed so easily! Sometimes when we kept Biscuit from going out, she'd get so frustrated she'd sit by the door and pull out her fur in mouthfuls, seizing up thatch after thatch of it with irate twists of her head. It looked agonizing. Coming back home was like walking into a barbershop, all this tawny hair strewn on the floor where she'd been sitting, like the pattern of iron filings that shows where a magnet was.

I understand that I'm ascribing to my cat the most human of human behaviors, the ascription of meaning. I'm imagining that the tilt of her head, the fixity of her gaze when she looked at me, signaled curiosity, or a particular disinterested variety of curiosity that might be called speculation. But can a cat speculate? Nobody questions that they're curious, but most evidence suggests that this curiosity is basically utilitarian, that when a cat stares at something, or sniffs it, or nudges it with a paw, climbs onto it or inside it, it's trying to fit the object of its curiosity into one of a limited number of conceptual slots, like the slots in an accordion file. Is this thing dangerous? That is, does it belong to the category of threats that may include other animals and, for some cats, human beings except for their owners (sometimes the owners too), along with moving cars, lawn mowers, and vacuum cleaners? Is this something I can eat? Is it something I can stalk and kill? Is it a female I can mount? (This asked by males.) Can I play with it? Is it something I can climb or hide in? The previously mentioned study of Kaspar Hauser cats indicates that some of these slots are present at birth, waiting to be filled by things their isolate, light-deprived owners may not even guess at.

Humans, too, have mental slots in which they file experience, and some humans have very few of them. We've all known people who view phenomena solely in terms of whether they can be eaten, screwed, or watched on a screen. But humans also possess another kind of curiosity for which the filing metaphor is inadequate, unless you picture an accordion file that contains an infinite number of slots, some of which are bottomless. And it's with this kind of curiosity that I imagine Biscuit watching me in the bathroom, wondering why I pull off my pelt and why that pelt changes from day to day, from rough to smooth or from slick to hairy, why sometimes it has a row of small hard nipples protruding from it, from which no milk comes, and why at other times the nipples are replaced by a sort of seam or scar that comes open with a soft, purring rasp.

But who am I kidding? When she looked at me, Biscuit probably saw the same thing the cat in the famous Kliban cartoon sees when it looks at a wall, as indicated by the thought bubble above its head: a wall.

In her case, it was a wall that moved and gave her food and love, though she might not know what love is. And I doubt it entered her mind that the wall told itself she loved it, too, educing as evidence the way she licked its hand in the morning and greeted it with an almost birdlike chirp when it came home from wherever it is a wall goes.

F. thinks that love is a specifically human emotion. She doesn't mean that only humans are capable of love but that only humans are really suited for it, and that when a domestic animal—a dog or a cat or one of the intelligent talking birds—learns to love, as it may from prolonged contact with a human being, it is almost always to its detriment. Sometimes that love is fatal to it.

Not long after we became involved, I had to go away to Southeast Asia for several weeks. The whole time I was gone, I missed F. as if she were the one who'd left and I were moping in the same dingy coffee shops I'd been moping in before I met her, for years. Nothing I saw overseas was exotic to me, not the rice paddies or the Buddhist temples shaped like enormous bells with young monks sitting on their steps in their orange robes, not the markets selling jackfruit big as fourth graders, not the crumpled shell of an American helicopter or the range where you could fire M-16s and AK-47s, depending on which set of combatants you felt like role-playing. It was just a landscape of subtraction. I came back diminished by a tropical infestation that wrung my guts like a washcloth. F. met me in my loft. She said I looked thin. We spent the day and evening in bed. Later we went to dinner. Because I was too weak to walk far, we chose a restaurant only a few blocks away. I don't know if it was sickness or love that made it so hard for me to eat. I'd raise my fork and watch it idle before my mouth. What was a fork for? This question wouldn't have occurred to a cat.

F. too appeared to be in rapture. She smiled across the table with shining eyes. But as I watched, a change came over her face; it seemed to melt and then re-form. Her smile became a smile of hatred, as cruel as that of an empress sitting in an arena and gazing down at men who were about to be slaughtered for her.

"Why are you looking at me that way?" I tried to keep the fear out of my voice, but a moment later I heard myself plead, "Don't look at me that way. I don't like it." I'm no longer sure of how she answered me. Maybe she said, "I wonder if you're really what you seem," or "I hope you don't turn out to be weak." She may have said, "I can't help myself. When I feel this way too long, I just want to bite." One thing I'm sure of is that she didn't pretend not to know what I was talking about. Between us lay the reality of that condemning smile. Both of us acknowledged it, though she may not have known the reason for it any more than I did.

At the time, I thought the smile meant she'd fallen out of love with me and hated me for it. I understood that feeling. The night D. proclaimed she loved me more than air, I cringed inwardly the way some people cringe from a street beggar, and a while later I was angry at her, the way people are at beggars. *Why doesn't somebody do something about them?* Years before, I'd felt the same anger at my girlfriend T., watching the meek curve of her shoulders as she sat before the TV in the apartment we shared in penury. I'm not sure if I was angry at her for tricking me into loving her or for letting me see her as she was, a bright, modestly pretty woman content with the modest pleasure of watching TV on a week night in a shitty apartment with a bathtub in the kitchen and burlap stapled to its rotten plaster walls. Falling out of love was so terrible that it had to be somebody else's fault. Why should F. be any different?

The Spanish verb *querer* means both "to love" and "to want." *Yo quiero* may be the beginning of a cry of sexual longing or of an order at the butcher counter. The same duality occurs in other languages, just not as blatantly. It defines love as a condition of insufficiency, a lack that can be cured only by the recovery of a missing object. Love is lovesickness. The lover is an open wound calling to the knife. In the *Symposium*, Plato has Aristophanes speak of that primeval race of compound beings—barrel shaped, eight limbed, with a face on either side of their spherical heads—whom the gods split in two "like a sorb-apple which is halved for pickling, or as you might divide an egg with a hair," so that forever after their cloven descendants wander the earth like ghosts, mourning what was taken from them: "Each of us when separated, having one side only, like a flat fish, is but the indenture of a man," Plato writes. What a terrible phrase that is, "the indenture of a man," a man bitten down to a stub. How can you not hate someone who reminds you of your indenturedness, especially when he is sitting across from you, close enough for you to see the tooth marks? Who made those marks?

On the day we were to begin living together, we found ourselves circling the Bronx in a fourteen-foot rental truck, searching for an alternate route to our new home after a cop herded us off the approach to the Taconic and told us the parkway is closed to commercial vehicles. Who knew our truck was a commercial vehicle? It wasn't like we were doing this to make money. Aghast at what we'd have to pay in the city, we'd decided to rent a house in the small town where F. lived. The truck was cavernous, or had been before we'd packed it. Now it was stuffed with stuff, mostly towers of crated books. My old roommate said the books were intellectual trophies and advised me to just take pictures of them and hang them on the walls of the new place, the way humane hunters pin up photos of the lions they didn't kill. He said it would make the move a lot easier. Of course, F.

muttered afterward, he didn't lift a finger to help us. We bumped and swayed alongside the river, whose steely glint on our left reassured us we were heading north. Then, suddenly we were crossing it. On a bridge! How had that happened? The bridge spilled us out in another state. "Where are we?" I asked F., but she couldn't read the map. She still can't read them. I knew we were supposed to be back on the other side of the river, but it was another half hour before I could turn around. And it was another two before we got to our new home, a two-story Dutch colonial covered in red aluminum siding that made it look like a toy caboose. Perched on its modest lawn, it seemed scarcely bigger than the truck we were about to offload into it.

We carried things inside, two small people, already middle-aged. The dining table wouldn't fit through the front door, and I couldn't find the screw gun I needed to take the top off the trestle base, so we left it on the lawn, figuring you could do that in the country but not realizing that when you do, you get a reputation as trailer trash. By the time we got to F.'s house, the light was fading. She had fewer things than I did, but many of them were still unpacked. Clocks, pictures, sofa cushions went into the truck piecemeal. On seeing us approach with her carrier, Tina began racing wildly about the apartment, almost panting in fear. When we finally scooped her inside and locked the gate behind her, she bashed against it till her nose bled. "Oh God!" F. cried. It was the most upset she got that day. If she was inclined to blame me—I was the one who locked the gate—she was grateful to me for getting rid of the decaying mole corpse she found in her pantry, where the little orange cat must have brought it in sometime before. It was my first experience with something far gone into putrefaction. I had to light a cigarette before I could bear to pick up the twist of blackened, half-liquefied matter with a paper towel. Having done this, I felt like a man. Which makes me wonder if there's something intrinsically manly about disposing of rotting corpses, even very small corpses, or if it's just about being able to do something that a woman can't or won't. Of course another woman might have disposed of those corpses perfectly well, even without a cigarette. But I'm not sure I could have fallen in love with her, or she with me.

We were still carrying F.'s things into the truck when it began to rain; the sound on the roof was deafening. For a while we huddled in the back, watching it smash down. It grew late, and we finished the move figuratively on tiptoes, like reverse burglars. Then we collapsed half-clothed onto a bed. In the morning we looked out the window and saw that the big maple on the front lawn had gathered all the red in the world into its foliage. It would be our tree. Its leaves would whisper to us as we slept or made love or read to each other in bed, and every fall we would rake them off the lawn and stuff them into big black trash bags. The only peace Ching would know in his haunted old age would be lying in front of it, staring at nothing. If only we could have buried his ashes there. But the ground was hard.

Looking down, I saw that the dining table was lying where we'd left it beside the door, its maple top spangled with rain.

For poor Tina, as I said, the house turned out to be a place of torment. From the moment she first picked up her scent, Bitey never missed an opportunity to put the fear of Cat into her. (I can only imagine what Tina felt when she saw the black beast send her human skidding down the stairs, seemingly just by looking at her.) There were moments when I thought F. would tell me that it was either her or Bitey. I don't know what I would have done then. You can give up a young cat for adoption, but who was going to adopt a middle-aged one that looked like Richard III and liked to bite the hand that petted her?

And the thing is, I loved her. I loved her as much as I would if I didn't have a girlfriend. I don't understand how that happened. In the beginning, I was alone and she was new, not just a new creature but a new phenomenon in my life, like a star that appears in a quadrant of the sky where no stars shone before. I'd grown up in a house without animals. My parents were European refugees, and like many Jews of their time and origin, they saw animals as dirty and a little scary: I'm not just talking about dogs, which it makes sense to be scared of if you come from a place where they were used to herd terrified humans into abattoirs, but, in my mother's case, cats. If one entered a room where she was sitting, she'd stiffen and grow pale. The cats I had when I was young were just ideas, probably inspired by a memory of a bleating pop song that used "two cats in the yard" as a metonymy of bohemian domestic bliss.

At first Bitey was an idea too: a companion animal, quieter than a dog and less demanding, requiring little more than food and water in her bowl and fresh litter in her box. But having nothing much better to do in those days, I spent a lot of time looking at her, and she became real. And because she was an animal, graced with an animal's self-absorption, she didn't mind my watching. She stretched as if I weren't there watching her. She stalked shadows and dust bunnies as if the world contained nothing but shadows, dust, and herself. She stared at walls. She hunkered in the cave of her being with slitted eyes, her forepaws tucked beneath her, her tail draped around her like an empress's stole, perfectly indifferent to the weight of my gaze. Love begins with looking, Proust tells us. I looked.

Bitey also went missing in September, late in the month, and I was terrified that she'd been snatched by a backwoods Satanist who was going to sacrifice her for Halloween. I don't know if we had real Satanists where we lived, but we had surly, thick-witted teenagers in Slipknot T-shirts who'd tell themselves they were Satanists as a pretext for setting an innocent house cat on fire, the same way earlier generations of surly thick-wits had told themselves they were Christians. How many miles I rode my bike in search of her, summoning her with the racket of IAMS "Adult Original with Chicken." "Bitey!" I called over and over. How many times in years to come F. and I would go about crying cats' names in loud, forlorn voices. People pretended not to stare at us from their porches, and we pretended not to see them staring.

A few weeks after we got her back, Bitey developed a sudden, terrible thirst. All night long she lapped from her bowl, frenetic and pop-eyed, then stumbled away like a drunk. When I took her to the vet the next morning, he thought it was diabetes. In the course of the day, the diagnosis kept changing. She had diabetes, but somehow it involved her liver. Then it wasn't diabetes. It might be cancer, but an X-ray showed no tumors. That evening F. and I came to see her and found her lying on her side on a steel table, emaciated—it had only been a day!—her eyes glazed. It was the first time I ever cried in front of F. She held me. Once I'd imagined that having someone to hold you when you were sad would be one of the benefits of marriage. But in the moment, it only felt embarrassing, and it didn't take away the fact that my cat was dying.

Actually, she wasn't dying, but it would be another week and $3,000 before I knew that. No one could ever say definitively what she'd had, what she *still* had when she came home with us, only that treating it involved feedings of a revolting prescription cat food that had to be blended with water into a grayish-brown slurry and then squirted into Bitey's mouth with a syringe, plus daily doses of a feline-strength formulary of the enzyme SAME, popular in Europe as an antidepressant, and daily administrations of subcutaneous fluids and antibiotics. The treatment was supposed to take a couple months. F. was away on a job, and I worried that I wouldn't be able to do it all myself. But Bitey was still weak and docile. All I had to do was sit down beside her on the bed, pet her a little to get her in the mood, then reach for the bag of fluid I'd hung from a ceiling hook, put a clean point on the line, and slip the point into the loose skin at her scruff. The worst part was the little pop of the incoming needle. I think it was that, rather than pain (cats don't have a lot of nerves back there), that sometimes made her start. For the next five minutes, I'd sit with her, scratching her ears as I watched a hundred milliliters of fluid drip from the bag and travel under her skin in a mouse-sized bulge before it was absorbed. About halfway through the procedure, I'd inject the antibiotic into a Y-port in the line. How astonishing that a doctor—even an animal doctor—had sold me a box of twenty-gauge syringes and that I was using those syringes on my cat and not myself. Bitey took it stoically. Only toward the end would she start growling. "Almost done," I'd tell her and give her a treat to keep her quiet a while longer.

Did she understand that this was for her own good? As long as we're talking about the threshold between human and animal, we might consider that humans are the only beings that seem to recognize that some kinds of painful and degrading treatment—injections, catheterizations, Hickman lines, CAT scans and MRIs, the shaving of head and pubic hair, enemas, colonoscopies, the splitting of thorax or abdomen and the plucking out of internal organs, which sometimes *are not put back*—that these ordeals, which any sentient creature might be expected to fly from howling, are beneficial to them. That the stickers and splitters have friendly intentions.

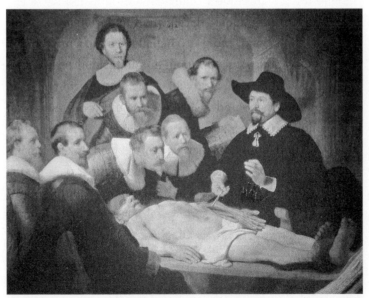

Rembrandt van Rijn, *The Anatomy Lesson of Dr. Nicolaes Tulp* (1632), Mauritshuis Museum, Amsterdam. Courtesy of the Bridgeman Art Library.

Children have to be taught this; it can take years. And even
grown-ups sometimes forget. A friend of mine, coming to after
a surgical procedure, began clawing at the lines in his hands,
wanting to know why he was being tortured. Later he said he
must have gone out of his mind for a while. But you might as
well say he'd momentarily come into his right one. In his delir-
ium, he'd broken free of the decades of indoctrination that
teach us to accept pain and humiliation as long as they're in-
flicted by strangers in lab coats.

F.'s father had also broken free of his indoctrination; I don't
know that it did him any good. He hadn't been to a doctor since
one had diagnosed him with chronic leukemia years before. He
didn't speak of people going to the hospital; he spoke of them
going to the slaughterhouse. "The bastards tell you they're taking you to the slaughterhouse for *some tests*, and that's the last
anybody hears of you."

We visited him the Christmas before we were married. He
and F.'s mother had divorced late, and he still hadn't gotten
over it. The dark condo with its brown carpeting unraveling
like a laddered stocking. The yellowing cards of Christmases
past arrayed on shelves and coffee table. The cheap cookware
that had never held anything but canned soup. They were the
marks of someone who either couldn't live by himself or had
chosen not to, preferring to stage the last years of his life as a reproach: to his faithless wife, to the children who didn't visit
him enough, to an entire world that knew nothing of his grief.
The resemblance between father and daughter was eerie,
down to the domed forehead and rabbit-like twitch of the nose.
F. had done her best to create a festive atmosphere. She'd gone

to the shopping center and come back with a spiral-cut ham whose slices fanned open like the pages of a book. "Isn't it nice, Daddy?" She presented him with a heaped plate that he barely glanced at. "I suppose." He said the ham wasn't as good as it used to be.

In former years, F.'s father had been prone to rages in which he'd rail at his wife and shove the children around. The threats he'd made sounded preposterous to me, but they must have been frightening and deeply embarrassing to three naive adolescent girls staring mutely as a red-faced grown-up told them that Castro was going to march in and shove his cigar up their asses. Now there was no trace of the old ferocity. His voice never rose above a murmur. Still, as we were talking in the kitchen, the refrigerator let out a squeal, probably something wrong with the fan, and abruptly the old man bared his teeth—bared them like an animal—and slammed it with the flat of his hand. "Bastard!" His eyes met mine for a moment, then looked away.

A few months after this, he fell ill. Probably he had been ill all that time but had refused to admit it. He couldn't eat, and he hurt everywhere. F. went down to Lexington to help care for him but, after a week, felt she had to go back to work. No sooner had her plane landed than she was suddenly struck by the certainty he was about to die. In a panic, she flew back once more and got there in time to sit by his bedside with her sisters as the last bit of life was twisted out of him.

During the time F.'s father was dying, I was sometimes petty with her. She was away, and I wanted her with me. She was sad and withdrawn, and I wanted her to be cheerful. Even now the memory of my behavior shames me. It also puzzles me. My mother had died only five years earlier, and for a long time afterward I'd walked through the world in a dream and bristled at any claim other people made on my attention; you'd think I would have understood what F. was going through. I've been told this amnesia isn't unique, and I can only relate it to the amnesia that comes over women after they give birth. The only way to bear this thing is to forget it. Of course, a woman who's had children can always choose not to have any more. But when it comes to death, you can't push away your plate and say, "No thanks, I couldn't eat another bite." The death kitchen goes on serving.

We put off our wedding six months. Late that spring we went back to Kentucky to clean out the old man's house. Before we left, we held a small memorial. I don't remember if F. bought another ham; it would have been fitting. But there was nice food, and wine and flowers, and we covered the dingy furniture with sheets, which produced an effect that was both austere and ethereal. Not many people came, apart from the family. At the climax of the afternoon, F. put on a tape we'd made of music he'd liked: a cut of a Scots marching band whose shrilling pipes lifted the hair on the back of your neck; the theme song of the old TV show *The Avengers*; some big band jazz he would have listened to as a young man on a last leave before shipping out for Italy, where most of his unit was wiped out at Anzio. From that same period, there was "I'll Be Seeing You," sung by Jo Stafford. Stafford's version may be the saddest song in the American songbook, saturated with yearning, slow as a dirge. Why does she sing it so slowly, you wonder? But, of course, "I'll Be Seeing You" is a song of the war years, and it's clear that Stafford is singing to a man who won't be coming back. She knows it, and he knows it. She's singing a love song for the dead. This accounts for the omnipresence of its object. The singer sees him everywhere—the children's carousel, the chestnut tree, the wishing well. Nothing like that happens when you just break up with somebody. In your imagination, she is where you know her to be: going out with an asshole she met at El Teddy's. Only the dead can be everywhere, and that's because they are nowhere.

I made the tape hastily, without EQ, so some tracks were much louder than others. Somehow I managed to lose several seconds of "Nessun Dorma." I hate to think what F.'s father would have said about that, but none of the guests seemed to really notice. F. and I may have been the only people there who were listening to the music as music rather than as the background for a gathering that couldn't decide whether it was sacred or social. F. said that her father would also have listened to the music as music and gotten angry with anyone who tried to talk over it. His remarks would have been restricted to a running commentary on the soundtrack: "'Nessun Dorma.' 'No one shall sleep.' From Puccini's immortal *Turandot*." But over time the commentary would have become increasingly emotional, until he was pacing the living room in agitation and, eventually, in rage.

The guests stole out until it was just F., her sisters, and me. The tape continued to play. The final track was a song F.'s father was unlikely to have listened to, Iggy Pop's snarling cover of "Real Wild Child." But F. had asked me to put it on the tape, feeling it expressed some aspect of his personality. Maybe it was the part of him that had bared his teeth in the kitchen, though I would have said that was just a passing convulsion of rage. You could imagine Iggy baring his teeth as he sang, but baring them the way you do when you're biting into a steak, a nice, thick, bloody one, the blood running down his chin. F. got up to dance, and I joined her. She's a terrific dancer, lithe and sexy and peppy and funny. One moment she'd be rolling her hips like a girl in a cage and the next she'd be prancing about on tiptoe, and she inspired me to be almost as uninhibited. It didn't occur to me that it might be inappropriate to dance at a memorial, especially the memorial of someone who, if he'd lived a few months longer, would have been my father-in-law. In former times, the Nyakyusa or Ngombe people of Tanzania were said to do this as a matter of practice, and their funerals, according to the anthropologist Monica Wilson, were correspondingly jolly:

> Dancing is led by young men dressed in special costumes of ankle bells and cloth skirts, often holding spears and leaping wildly about. Women do not dance, but some young women move about among the dancing youths, calling the war cry and swinging their hips in a rhythmic fashion. . . . The noise and excitement grow and there are no signs of grief. Yet when Wilson asked the onlookers to explain the scene, they always replied, "They are mourning the dead."

Turandot is Puccini's last opera. He died before he could finish it, and it was given its present ending by a second composer. When the opera was first performed at La Scala, on April 25, 1926, the orchestra fell silent in the middle of the third act, and the conductor Arturo Toscanini is said to have laid down his baton and addressed the audience: "Qui finisce l'opera lasciata incompiuta dal Maestro, perchè a questo punto il Maestro è morte" ("Here ends the opera left incomplete by the Maestro, because at this point the Maestro died"). The curtain fell.

F. and I almost postponed our wedding a second time, since a few days before it was supposed to take place a pair of hijacked jetliners crashed into the World Trade Center. After a day or two of indecision—during which we fretted about how petty it was to even be thinking about a wedding when almost 3,000 of our neighbors had just been murdered before our eyes—we were persuaded to go ahead: our friends who lived in the city said they *needed* us to go ahead. As one of them put it, "I need a party to go to." If I'd had any real doubts, I might have been swayed by the stories of the people who jumped from the burning towers holding hands. I don't know if any of them were married to each other; some of them may have been lovers, as often happens in workplaces. For months and years, they'd kept their relation secret, but in a matter of minutes the need for secrecy was over, and they jumped together, in full view of the world, holding hands. A man and a woman leaping off a burning building while holding hands struck me as a metaphor for marriage, the clause in the vow that goes "till death shall us part." But this probably says something about my laziness and the shortness of my attention span. It took only ten seconds for the people who jumped from the World

Trade Center to hit the ground, and that's not a long time to
hold hands.

~~~

I could tell I was nearing the airport when I began to pass
beachfront lined with condos that leaned contemptuously over
the undeveloped real estate of the Atlantic. What must the tenants who lived to seaward feel when they stepped out onto their
balconies? Satisfaction at their unobstructed view of white sand
and blue-green water or irritation that they had to share it with
their neighbors or, worse, the tiny freeloaders strolling down the
public beach with zinc oxide on their noses? Across the highway were golf courses and an amusement park full of
corkscrewing waterslides and a Medieval Times restaurant. Curious about what a medieval menu would look like—larks'
tongues? chine of beef?—I later checked out the online reviews. One visitor said the dungeon had been a letdown.

I parked and walked to the terminal. It was almost sunset
but still warm. The passengers at the ticket counter wore shorts
and sandals and were tanned various reddish browns. I'm sure
I was too; I tan easily. If I ran into people I knew when I got up
north, they'd exclaim at how good I looked. Up there, it would
already be getting cold, and some mornings there'd be frost on
the ground. If I were still living at home, I'd be harvesting the
late vegetables. Biscuit liked to watch me do that. On seeing
me head for the yard with a spade and hand rake, she'd follow
me closely, which used to puzzle me until I realized she was
probably waiting to see if I'd dig up any small rodents. You see
what a clever cat she was. She'd sniff the roots I tugged from

the ground, plump and matted with earth. But she always turned away. They were only beets, and what could be less interesting to a cat than a dirty beet?

~~~

Bitey was never the same after her illness. She still enjoyed menacing Tina but could no longer do it with her old élan. After one assault, F. lost patience with her and, seizing her by the back of the neck, dragged her the length of the kitchen, meaning to lock her in the basement as punishment. She knew better than to try picking her up, but there was a time when she wouldn't even have been able to scruff her. Bitey screamed in protest, her limbs splayed impotently on the tiled floor. Probably compounding her wretchedness was the fact that Suki was following her closely and sniffing her butt, and Tina, her intended victim, was watching with interest. A humiliated cat probably emits a special tincture of shame that its fellows find deeply pleasurable.

Some months later, while I was petting her, she bit my hand with more than usual ferocity. She wouldn't release me. She just glowered up at me with those absinthe-colored eyes; it really hurt. At last I gave her a swat, and she sprang away. But one of her fangs remained lodged in the meat between my thumb and forefinger. It stayed there only a moment, then fell out by itself. Not long after this, she died.

As I held her in the vet's office, she cried in fear. The sound was like a small horn playing a single plaintive note. No amount of soothing could make her stop. The vet said Bitey might be hallucinating. Of course, you hear of humans doing that at the end, as they pass into what may be the next world or one of the worlds they traveled through on their way to this moment. On his deathbed F.'s father called out for his mother. She'd died when he was a small boy, disappearing into the hospital to be treated for something no one bothered to explain to him and never coming home. How long had it been since he'd called her name? All those people we keep folded inside us, filed away like old deeds. We can't bear to throw anything away. As awful as it was that my cat was dying, it seemed worse to me that she was dying in fear. "It's okay, honey," I kept murmuring to her as she let out those monotonous dying calls and stared in horror at a spot on the ceiling above my left shoulder. "You're safe, you're safe." I don't think it could be called lying. A cat has no way of knowing what "safe" means.

In my closet I have a box of letters I collected from my mother's apartment after her death. Many of them are written on that ethereal blue aerogram stationery that signifies foreign travel far more than a postcard of the Colosseum or a camel can, as well as the frugality of a time when people worried about the weight of a letter. Some of the letters are from her parents, written during the war when my mother first came to this country from Europe. Some were written later on, when she was traveling. Some are from me. I found an entire bundle of the ones I used to send her from summer camp. I rarely had much to say. Today I caught a fly ball (which was probably a lie). We had crafts; I made an ashtray. There are letters from my mother's cousins, the ones in Boston, the ones in Moscow, the ones in Tel Aviv, the one in Winnipeg whom she held in

awe because he wasn't just rich but a lawyer and not just a lawyer but a "solicitor," a "Queen's counsel." The way she fawned
over him used to drive me crazy.

At the time I emptied my mother's apartment, I took out as
many as five boxes of letters. But over the years I culled them
the same way I culled her other papers, throwing out state-
ments from long-closed bank accounts, instruction manuals
for appliances that had broken years before. I used to go
through her letters every year or so, when there was something
else I was trying to avoid doing. In this way, I was able to get rid
of the ones I thought ephemeral or meaningless. Still, many
letters, especially the older ones, are in foreign languages—
German, Russian, Swedish—and I can't bring myself to get rid
of them until I know what they say. They may turn out to be as
inconsequential as the ones I chucked: thank-yous for wedding
or baby presents, records of long-ago holidays when nothing
happened. We went to the museum of arms and armor. Emil
was deeply interested in the arbalests. Munich turned out to be
foggy and unseasonably cool. Your uncle was struck by the
number of soldiers in the streets. But they may say more than
that. I keep promising myself to get them translated.

After Bitey died, I was in no hurry to adopt another cat. I
was surprised at how sad I was. Every time I entered a room, I
looked down reflexively and was stricken not to see her. The
entire house became suffused with her absence. It was almost
the opposite of what happens in "I'll Be Seeing You." I saw her
nowhere. The bed was a bed without her on it; the armchairs
were empty of her. The dining table had no black cat lounging
on a heap of mail, waiting to scatter it when she was shooed

off. It was more constant, more *preoccupying*, than any grief I'd known before. A month after my father's death, I'd flown to Paris to hook up with a girlfriend who'd gone overseas for graduate studies. It was just before New Year's and very cold, the streets around Les Halles powdered with light snow. Almost from the moment of my arrival, I'd figured out that L. had lost interest in me, and my disappointment displaced whatever else I was feeling. Every few blocks I'd have to stop in a bar for an Armagnac and a coffee, the coffee to disguise the Armagnac, make it look like some species of creamer served in a balloon glass. Only after I came back home did I remember that my father had lived in Paris for a few years before the war; he'd gotten out just before the Germans marched in. The whole time I was there, it never entered my mind. Looking back, I see an inverse symmetry between my response to my cat's death and my response to my father's: In one case, the lost object remained constantly present in my consciousness, which made the object's absence from the world more acute, more haunting. In the other case, the lost object had vanished not just from the world but from the field of my attention, and to such a degree that I passed through a city that had once been associated with the object—had once been home to it, to him—without that connection ever rising to consciousness.

Can we speak of some lost objects as being more lost than others?

Oddly, for all the times I was reminded of my cat's absence, I half believed that she was still there in the house. Some of this was because of how the other cats had behaved when F. and I came back from the vet's office where we'd sat with Bitey

at the end. Instead of greeting us at the door, the two gray tab-
bies, Suki and Ching, gazed fixedly down at us from the top of
the stairs. When I climbed up to where they were sitting, they
continued to stare past me. "What are they looking at?" F.
asked from below. I turned to follow their gaze. All I saw was
the floor of the vestibule, with its scuffed boards and inexpertly
lined-up shoes. Suddenly I knew it was Bitey. "If it's you," I
called, "come in. Please. You're welcome here."

I suppose that belief, which wasn't really a belief but a
more forceful kind of wish, was what made me keep looking
for Bitey in every room I entered for weeks after her death.
Whatever the impulse was, it wasn't wholly mistaken. To keep
the lost object in mind is to keep it alive. You hold it cupped in
consciousness as you might cup a lit match in your hands to
keep it from being blown out in the wind. This, according to
the philosopher George Berkeley, is what God does with the
entire universe, each of whose trillions of objects, down to its
tiniest grains of matter, exists only because the Creator has
thought of it, is thinking of it, sustaining it from moment to
moment with the labor of his enormous and encyclopedic
brain. I find this idea very moving, even though I have a hard
time believing, as Berkeley did, that there is no such thing as
matter. But then, Berkeley, who was also an Anglican bishop,
seems to have felt that it was only a short step from believing in
the existence of matter to disbelieving the existence of God.
You can imagine what he might've felt about appointing gays
and lesbians to the clergy.

Berkeley is an example of somebody whose ideas are consistent. Mine are not. I grieved for my cat even as I nursed the

fantasy that she was still present in our house in a small town in the Hudson Valley, where F. and I had moved when we began to have faith in our relationship, this third thing that had arisen between us, as if from the vapor of our breath, and then condensed, the way your breath condenses on a window pane, so that you can write a name in it. The consequences of these beliefs were the same. On sad days, I could barely pay attention to the surviving cats. On days when my spirits were higher, I worried that getting a new cat would be unseemly. Thinking about the etymology of that word, its roots in "seeming" and "seeing," I ask myself who or what might have been offended to see a new cat romping around our home. But, of course, I know the answer. I was thinking of Bitey. Bitey would see.

In many stories of the supernatural, a ghost is summoned back by jealousy, a fury at being replaced.

Here I mention that for a long time after her father's death, F. would lay out a small plate for him at mealtimes, placing on it small portions of the foods he used to like: olives, nuts, cheese, a bite of meat or fish. Sometimes she'd set out a fancy gold-rimmed goblet in which she'd pour a single swallow of wine. She, or maybe her father, favored reds. And the last time I visited my mother's grave, I brought along not the usual flowers but a box of chocolates, an expensive gift assortment. I waited till I was about to leave, then set the box down by her headstone. I may have said, "Here, this is for you." I haven't been back since, and maybe that's because some part of me doesn't want to know if the chocolates are still there.

7

THE ANNOUNCEMENTS THAT ECHOED THROUGH THE wide spaces of Myrtle Beach International Airport made me think of death. It was the way they alternated warning and invitation. "If you are carrying more than three ounces of any liquid, gel, or cream, please place it in a Ziploc bag and put it in a receptacle." "All Gold Club members, passengers with special needs, or passengers with small children are welcome to board at this time." "Do not accept any item given to you by a person unknown to you." I had a picture—I was probably remembering it from a movie—of some antechamber of The Forever where angels sort out the new arrivals before herding them to their respective gates, Gold Club or Economy, praising the virtuous and hectoring the damned.

I've never been especially scared of my plane crashing. What I'm scared of is the minute before: the unending, spiraling fall in which I'll either be spun about the cabin or mashed into my seat with my face warped in an Iroquois mask of disbelieving terror, cheeks skinned back from my teeth. I'm scared I may scream. I'm scared I may piss myself, and be seen screaming and pissing myself. For years, I forestalled this potentiality by telling God that if it was between sending the plane down and killing me with a heart attack, he could give me the heart attack. The hope was he'd think I was making the offer out of concern for my fellow passengers. Sometimes I expressed it as a prayer, especially once during a lurching flight from Ho Chi Minh City to Vientiane in a Chinese-built prop plane that seemed to plunge 1,000 feet every time we passed over a gap in the mountains. Most of the other passengers were families with small children, and in my address I made a big deal about that, murmuring, "For the sake of these innocents," in a ripe interior voice that would have sickened a Republican presidential candidate.

On October 2, as the plane taxied down the runway, then flung itself into the air, I changed my prayer. *Please get me home safely so I can find my little cat.*

The setting sun sent its fire through the windows. The hair on my arms was incandescent; the woman sitting beside me might have been made of brass. Looking down, I could see a path of light spreading across the ocean. I don't believe in a god who responds to petitions. What is God, a mayor? The truth is, I never cared that much about the other passengers, not even those adorable Laotian kids.

~ ~ ~

One of the things F. and I still agree about is that it started going bad after we moved from the house on Parsonage Street. Maybe it was just that our lives were simpler there, in the mechanical sense. Living in the village, we could walk or bike to shops and restaurants or, when Wilfredo was visiting, down to the little public park to feed the ducks that paddled up and down the slow-moving creek. We didn't argue about who was using the car. We were content with simple entertainments, especially reading aloud, whole books straight through, none of this PoMo skipping over the boring parts. F. is an expressive reader, and her interpretation of certain characters approached genius. One night we were doing the scene in *Oliver Twist* in which Bumble the Beadle is putting the make on Mrs. Corny, the grasping workhouse matron. "Are *you* a weak creetur?" he asks her meaningfully. I may have put a hand on F.'s thigh. She looked over her shoulder at me in a way that was at once flirtatious and reproving, and she read the next line not like somebody pretending to be modest but like somebody who on reflection realizes that she actually *is* modest, who knew? She lowered her eyes. "We are *all* weak creeturs."

The cats were safe on Parsonage Street, if you discount one of them disappearing for a month, which was awful for us but for Bitey was probably an adventure. Because the street dead-ended, we could let Biscuit loll on the warm asphalt of the road beside the yard. Nobody minded slowing down or even coming to a stop if she didn't care to get up. She'd lie there, turn her head to see what was making the noise behind her, then go back to licking her paw, and usually the driver would just back up and steer around her. Sometimes he'd give a short tap on the horn, as if to say, "Ta-ta."

I used to complain about how dowdy our house was, but the dowdiness suited us. It curbed our (or maybe I should say my) grandiosity, reminding us (or me) that we lived in a house that had carpeting on its stairs and blue-and-white shepherds and shepherdesses minueting on the wallpaper: F. must have seen them minueting as she skidded past them down the stairs. For the same reason, it helped that only a small yard separated our house from our neighbors'. Day after day, we did more or less the same things in our yard as they did in theirs: we brought in bags of groceries and put out bags of trash; we planted flowers and vegetables and weeded the beds with the hoe we'd bought at The Phantom Gardener; we grilled salmon on a rusty Weber while playing music on the stereo. When we cooked, we listened to Garbage and Sonic Youth. The people behind us played a C&W station. The music was cheerful; those boinging pedal steels made me think of the Looney Tunes theme. But the male voices were thick with self-pity, and the words often seemed to be about dropping a bomb someplace or punching somebody in the mouth for questioning your right to do it. Well, I doubt the neighbors were any crazier about Kim Gordon. I used to imitate the husband ordering their small dog to "go peepee, go peepee!" F. and I argued about whether he could hear me. I always said he couldn't, but for all I know, while Toby Keith was hollering, "We'll put a boot in your ass, it's the American way," the neighbor was imitating us calling our cats in babyish voices. "Bitey! Ching! Tina! Biscuit!" What kind of dumbass is dumb enough to think a cat's going to come if you call it?

Almost the first thought that came to me when I learned Biscuit had gone missing was that this would never have happened if we'd stayed in our old home. I don't mean just for

practical reasons but for moral ones. We were being punished
for wanting a bigger house with more land around it, for wanting not to have to listen to our neighbors' music. We were being punished for wanting to live like gentry instead of tenants.

I know F. felt something like that when we lost Gattino.

At the time, it didn't feel like we were getting above ourselves.
We'd been on Parsonage Street for almost eight years. The
house had gotten cluttered; the boxes we'd stored in the basement had grown coats of mold. One autumn the landlord got
ambitious and had the red siding peeled off and replaced with
the beige vinyl he used on his other houses. His workers
strewed the yard with red aluminum shrapnel and tufts of
bubblegum-colored insulation; all our flowers died. What had
been wrong with our red aluminum? When we got an offer to
rent a bigger place in the next town to the north, we jumped at
it. The property had a barn and a big garden with lilac trees
and peonies—beautiful peonies, as big and fluffy as cockatoos.
The landlord was a friend of friends. At the time I was dumb
enough to think of that as an asset.

Maybe it was the prospect of moving that put me in an
expansive mood. F. was going to a residency in Italy that summer, and we decided I'd meet her afterward so we could
spend two weeks driving through the country between Tuscany and Rome. It would be our first vacation since our hon-
eymoon and the first real trip we'd taken together to another
country. I don't count the time we'd gone to Russia two years
before because that was for work and its picturesque high
point, a midnight boat ride down the canals of St. Petersburg,

ended with F. hitting her head on the underside of a low bridge and getting a concussion. There's a photo I took of her just moments before the collision, which, mercifully, was slow and very soft, a stone tap. In it, she gazes over the tops of her glasses at something just beyond the frame, her skin translucent, her hair spectrally pale. Her expression is at once intent and vague, the expression of someone peering through a mist with such concentration that she fails to see the solid object that's about to rear out of its depths and smack her on the head.

At the time we made our travel plans, I had no job to speak of and was already in debt. Looking back, I wonder what I was thinking. Probably, I was thinking of being a lover again rather than a husband. The word "husband" means both a male spouse and, in its verb form, to use resources economically, to conserve. I bought a $700 plane ticket; I booked hotel rooms that cost €100 a night. This was not husbandry. It's true I spent that money with the aim of making F. happy, but a wife's happiness may not really be a husband's business. His business is to take care of her, to ensure she has fuel to make a fire with and meat to cook on it and a roof to keep off the rain. It's to protect her and their children from every danger that a malignant world might launch at them. It's to be the guarantor of her modesty. Neither Adam nor Abraham tried to make their women happy—when Sarah laughed, she laughed out of incredulity and bitterness—and if you had suggested that they ought to, they, too, would have laughed, except they would have been laughing at you. Changes in the husband's role seem to have been underway by early in the Christian era, for Paul says that a married man will care for the things of this world "that he may please his wife" (I Cor. 7:33). This is why he thought men ought to be celibate.

Making a woman happy is the task of a lover. Considered purely as labor, this isn't as hard as having to see to her well-being and safety, but it requires paying close attention to things that are unquantifiable, even invisible—to shades, nuances, emanations. Good lovers seem to have internal receptors that detect the most spectral traces of female longing and pleasure: I don't mean just the sexual kind. One may think of those receptors as a counterpart to the vomeronasal organs cats deploy in flehmen, the open-mouthed sneer with which they take in interesting odors.

A cat's sensors are designed to assess scent signals from a variety of sources, but a lover focuses his powers on a single object or on the class of which that object is a member: a woman or women. From moment to moment, often quite un-consciously, he trains his attention on the object to determine what she wants from him: a back rub, some home-baked bread, lingerie, chocolate, poetry, a sympathetic ear, a comforting shoulder, a hard dick. Some men understand the value of these things; others snort, What bullshit! Isn't it enough I change the fucking oil? It may be that marriage began its pres-ent slide at the point when husbands decided that they too needed to be lovers. Some will say that women first gave them the idea, but it was probably someone in magazine publishing or a florist or a manufacturer of toiletries who was looking for a way to make men buy cologne. And let's not forget the makers of ribbed condoms.

During the time F. was alone in Italy and I was waiting to join her, she took in a small kitten. She found it in the yard of a derelict farmhouse near the residency, where she was steered by one of the staff. "Do you like little cats?" this woman may have asked, in the manner of pimps everywhere. "I have some adorable ones to show you." The kitten was very sick, its nose gummed with secretions, its belly hard and swollen with worms. When F. picked it up, which she could do because it was weaker than its littermates, she saw that it was blind in one eye. At first, she meant only to have it treated by a local vet be-fore releasing it back in the farmyard to gambol gauntly with its brothers and sisters. But over the weeks in which she kept it in her rooms, dosing it with the medicines the vet had given her, she became attached to it. And the kitten, which early on had viewed her with a feral creature's wary pragmatism, grew attached to her. She told me about it in phone calls. Yesterday the kitten had followed her about with its tail raised. Today while she was working, it had climbed into her lap and teethed on her fingers. Last night he had slept with her. I noted the change of pronoun. Then F. told me she wanted to bring him back to the States. She said she loved him. More important, the kitten loved her, seemingly in violation of his— its—nature. She had taught him love, or maybe infected him with it, and if she left him back at the farm, she was scared he'd be stuck with this feeling that was too big for him, that was too big for most humans, and he would suffer. My heart sank. It was so typical of F.'s love, which is so often called forth by an apprehension of the object's doom. Why couldn't she have fallen for a kitten that was healthy and saw out of both eyes, an American kitten? But then I suggested a name for him: Gattino. This is a stupid thing to do with a creature you don't want to get attached to.

I got to the residency late in the afternoon, after driving four hours from Milan in a rented Lancia on roads that wound around the hillsides like a long caress. I parked in front of a low stone tower and got out of the car. F. ran into my arms. She glowed as if suffused by the sun. Her hair and skin were golden. She smelled of rosemary. Gattino was waiting in her bedroom. On seeing me, he scrambled under a dresser, and I had to kneel down and talk to him soothingly before he would come out. He had long legs—he was going to be a big cat—and his veiled eye and big, blunt nose gave him a look of jaunty toughness, like one of those skinny Neapolitan kids who grows up to be a prizefighter or a gigolo. He prowled the table, sniffing my wallet and car keys, then lay down with us on the bed. That night, he slept on top of me, purring.

There was no question of taking him with us while we traveled, and for a while I worried that F. would want to call off the trip. She was afraid to leave Gattino at the vet's. She was afraid he wouldn't be cleared for immigration or importation, I'm not sure what to call it. I know he needed to be given a clean bill of health, and there was some doubt he'd get one. He was still frail, and there was that eye. The clinic was crowded, filled with the acridness of caged animals and their outcries of fear, hunger, and anger. An attendant placed Gattino in a cage next to one holding a large dog, bristling with muscle, that barked and slavered. Gattino cried. F. began crying too. I'd seen her cry only once or twice since her father's death, maybe over Wilfredo. But who wouldn't cry, seeing a kitten placed in a cage beside an immense dog that wanted nothing more than to eat his small heart? Even here, though, you could see his spirit. Instead of cowering, our cat (already I was thinking of him as ours) peered out at his tormentor with an intrepid forward tilt of his ears. His tail was lowered, but it wasn't tucked between his legs. It was out behind him, and this made him look as if he were about to launch himself forward like an arrow at a target. At the very least, he would hold his ground.

For the next two weeks, I was F.'s lover again. We drove as fast as you can drive in a little car without scaring yourself into incompetence; out of the corner of my eye, I could see my wife's bare feet propped on the dashboard, and the casualness of her posture reassured me that I wasn't about to get us killed.

We walked hand in hand through the cobbled defiles of hillside towns, up stone steps whose sheerness put us in an allegorical frame of mind. There was usually a cathedral at their summit, and above its spires the same blue sky where Signorelli saw angels swooping. We stood on battlements, looking out at wheat fields and grape vineyards that had provisioned the Borgias while the shadows of clouds lengthened over them, turning the rows of grain a dull bronze. We sat in restaurants whose white linen glowed in the candlelight; surely all those restaurants can't have been candlelit, but in retrospect it seems that way. Each dish was fundamental. It tasted of the elements that had produced it, tomatoes of earth and sun, a roasted dorado of fire and the sea. The waiters masqueraded as layabouts. All evening they looked at the pretty girls on the next terrace or an especially slick motor scooter or a platoon of German tourists uniformly burned the color of raw salmon—at anything but you until the moment you wanted something, at which point they appeared at your side and said, "Mi dica." We hung out beside fountains that might have been the originals for the fountains where I hung out as a teenager, out past curfew, looking for a girl to be with, and now at last, thirty-five years later, here I was, with her.

Most of the pictures I took in those places are pictures of her.

Among literary forms, the lyric is the lover's mode, for that's how a lover experiences the world, as a series of isolated moments bright with feeling, like stills from a movie whose intervening frames have been excised. The world starts with the love object, and it ends with her. Whatever else it contains—sun, moon, stars, a blue flower, a blanket crumpled on the grass, a dark wood—exists only to reflect the loved one or otherwise call attention to her, or to what she evokes in the lover. The sun and moon are the bodies whose light he sees her by; the stars are the jewels he would give her if only he could climb into the sky to quarry them; the blue flower is what he gives her in their place. The blanket is where he lies with her on the grass on a summer evening, the first fireflies bursting silently in the still air. He sees them out of the corner of his eye. The rest of the time he is looking at her.

The lyric is beset with paradox. The moment it evokes may be brief as a heartbeat, yet it seems to go on forever, an eternity in which Sappho can raptly take account of everything that is happening inside her:

> . . . if I meet
> you suddenly, I can't
> speak—my tongue is broken;
> a thin flame runs under
> my skin; seeing nothing,
>
> hearing only my own ears
> drumming, I drip with sweat;
> trembling shakes my body
>
> and I turn paler than
> dry grass.

In Gerald Stern's "Another Insane Devotion," the narrator's
sudden, shattering encounter with one of Rome's ravenous
street cats frames an entire history of lost love:

> . . . I have
> told this story over and over; some things
> root in the mind; his boldness, of course, was frightening
> and unexpected—his stubbornness—though hunger
> drove him mad. It was the breaking of boundaries,
> the sudden invasion, but not only that it was
> the sharing of food and the sharing of space; he didn't
> run into an alley or into a cellar,
> he sat beside me, eating, and I didn't run
> into a trattoria, say, shaking,
> with food on my lips and blood on my cheek, sobbing;
> but not only that, I had gone there to eat
> and wait for someone. I had maybe an hour
> before she would come and I was full of hope
> and excitement. I have resisted for years
> interpreting this, but now I think I was given
> a clue, or I was giving myself a clue,
> across the street from the glass sandwich shop.
> That was my last night with her, the next day
> I would leave on the train for Paris and she would
> meet her husband. Thirty-five years ago
> I ate my sandwich and moaned in her arms, we were
> dying together; we never met again . . .

One moment stands in for other moments or contains them, hundreds, thousands, a lifetime of moments curled inside that one like the strands of DNA inside the nucleus of a cell. What makes that possible is memory. Memory stretches out for fifty-seven lines the moment in which the poet eats beside the starving creature to which he's surrendered a scrap of his sandwich and packs within that interval days and nights of lovemaking and a lifetime of reckoning and regret. Unless it's literally written in the moment, scrawled between kisses on a cocktail napkin on the nightstand, the lyric is a memory masquerading as the lived present. And its beauty is that it feels like the present: it feels more like now than now does.

A further paradox is that the lyric, although inspired by love for another person, often leaves that person in shadow. All Sappho tells us about her beloved is that her voice is a sweet murmur and her laughter is enticing. Of Stern's we know this: she was married, or was about to be; they floated naked in the sea and moaned in each other's arms; she was going to have a baby; it was his. This isn't much. And yet Stern's lover haunts his poem as Sappho's lover haunts Sappho's, manifested in one poet's outrushing of memory and the other's burning speechlessness. Both poets evoke a hidden object by registering her effect on them. In the same way, by measuring the perturbations in a star's orbit, astronomers can determine the existence of a black hole.

My favorite photo of that summer is one I took of F. in Volterra. There was some wind that day, and her long hair is blowing about her face. It was F. who showed me that if you cover one half of a face in a photograph, its expression changes, sometimes so dramatically that you seem to be looking at an entirely different face, animated by feelings that are barely discernible in the original. If you move your hand to the other side, still another face appears. In the photo I'm speaking of, F. seems, if not happy, confident in her loveliness. Her gaze meets the camera boldly. But when I cover the left side of her face, the other half turns watchful and melancholy, with a nostril dilated as if from crying. And when the experiment is reversed, the half face that peers out from behind your hand is taut with defiance, as if she were daring you to breach her privacy, and the half smile that tugs at the corner of her mouth is devoid of pleasure.

It was Rome that F. liked best. It was more alive than Florence or Siena; it didn't just unroll its past and invite you to sample it. It gave you sexy teenage couples horsing around amid the ruins, a mezzo with no chin and a tubby baritone singing arias in a church. F. marveled at their plainness. She loved it that people so plain could enact desire frankly, without apologizing, eyes flashing, bellies heaving. Yet, even in Rome, she was tormented by thoughts of Gattino. She prayed for him in churches. She called the veterinary clinic to ask if he was eating. She worried that the vet wouldn't be able to get him cleared for travel: there were rumors of bad blood between him and the regional official—the head veterinarian of the entire region of Tuscany—who was supposed to sign the papers. The airline specified that cats could only travel in-cabin in carriers of certain strict dimensions, and nowhere could we find one the right size. The variety of merchandise in the pet shops was jaw-dropping. There were cat carriers covered in soft leather and rip-stop nylon, cat carriers belted like trench coats. All displayed the Italian genius for design, but all were off by centimeters in one or more dimensions. F. took it as a bad sign. "They won't let him on the plane." I told her they would. "They're Italians, sweetheart, they don't give a shit about bureaucracy." But even as I said this, I remembered that they had also more or less invented it. I think it was the Romans who came up with the first initialism.

S.P.Q.R.

We drove back to Tuscany and reclaimed Gattino from the clinic. He looked more robust, his nose was dry, and when we presented him to the provincial vet, he stepped out of his new carrier as if he expected to be admired. But the provincial vet looked at him disapprovingly; he didn't look at us at all. The cat, he said, was too sick to travel. Our vet, who had come there with us, argued with him—politely, he was conscious of the man's power. His hands made soft, beckoning gestures. The official kept shaking his head. "No, no, no." He may have said, "I don't have time for this." F. looked as if she might faint. I blurted something in Italian: "Senza la mia moglie e me, questo piccolo gattino non ha nessun' amico in tutta l'Italia!" ("Except for my wife and me, this little kitty doesn't have one friend in all Italy!") Both vets looked at me, but it accomplished nothing. Well, it embarrassed F., and that may have distracted her a little from her unhappiness.

On leaving the interview, our vet told us that he would go to Umbria the next day and have *their* head vet stamp Gattino's passport. It would be no problem, he assured us: the vet was a friend of his. And when he gave them to us just before we left, we saw that Gattino's papers really did look like a passport.

They even had the same burgundy cover the EU uses on the ones it issues human beings.

~~~

I spent an hour or so in the sky, gazing down at the profile of the continent and nodding and smiling as the woman next to me, who had turned from brass back to soft, perishable flesh, told me about the grandchild who was about to be produced in time for her arrival. When I told her I was going up to New York to search for a missing cat, she looked at me with what I was pretty sure was pity. Was it pity for someone who was looking for something he was extremely unlikely to find or pity for someone who had no better outlet for his affections than a cat? "Well, *good luck*," she said. It was as if I'd told her I was on my way to have surgery for a brain tumor. I thanked her.

~~~

Husbands have written lyrics, but they aren't really suited for it. The lyric form can't express the state of being a husband, for that is not about feeling but being. A man becomes a husband by saying, "Till death do us part," or, if he's squeamish about the d-word, "As long as we both shall live." In either case, he rarely knows what he's getting into. Feeling is brief; being has duration. A husband can feel many things, but he *is* one thing, and he may go on being that thing long after the feelings that brought him to it have passed. What feeling lasts a lifetime, except maybe statistically, the tissue-thin temporal slices of love stacking up higher than those of irritation, dislike, even hatred by so many microns that measuring those stacks at the end you can plausibly say, *We were happy*? Or *I was*?

Being a husband is also about action, which is why the husband's ideal literary form is narrative. *The Odyssey*, which is sometimes reckoned the first novel, is the story of a husband who's trying to get back to his wife. Most husbands don't have to do as much as Odysseus does to accomplish this, or for as long, and they don't get to do it with cute nymphs and a princess. They go out on the day's errands, buy some things for the missus, and stop at the fitness center for a sauna. There's a funeral where they have to pay respects. They make some business calls, have a little lunch. At a fund-raising event, a mean drunk tries to pick a fight with them; they leave shaken. Later, around the time they ought to be going home, they run into another drunk. It's the son of an old friend, grown up since they last saw him but he hasn't learned how to hold his liquor yet, and knowing the kinds of grief a drunk kid can get into, they tag along with him as he weaves in and out of every dive and blind pig in the city, even a whorehouse. God knows what would happen to the little dipshit if they weren't around to keep an eye on him. It's late, and the kid's still shwacked, so they take him home to crash on the sofa. The wife's asleep in the bedroom, or maybe pretending to be. No way of telling if she's mad at them for coming home so late or. So they lie down beside her, and in a while they fall asleep too. Change a few particulars and you have *Ulysses*.

In narrative, order is crucial, chronological order especially. Consider how that story would read if the husband stopped by the house before the unpleasantness with the drunk. Consider an *Odyssey* in which the hero comes home in the first twenty

pages, kills the suitors, then leaves again to make time with Ca-
lypso. Sequencing is also essential to husbandry. A husband
plows before he sows. He pays the rent before the premium ca-
ble. He buys heating oil before he buys a snowblower, though it
would be nice to have one, especially after pulling his back like
he did shoveling out the driveway last winter and getting a case
of sciatica that his wife charmingly kept calling "ass-leg." He
doesn't book an Italian vacation before he finds a job or collects
an advance from his publisher, and certainly not a month
before he and his wife are supposed to move to another house.
Before leaving the underground parking garage in a scenic village famed for its museum of Etruscan artifacts (and, he later
learns, for its appearance in Stendhal's *On Love*), he makes sure
he knows where the ticket is so that later he doesn't have to
spend a quarter of an hour futilely slapping his pockets while
behind him a queue of Italian cars grows longer and longer and
their drivers honk at him in mounting, polyphonic fury. Before
changing his return flight so that he can escort his wife and her
new kitten from Florence to Milan, he demands more than a
customer service representative's assurance over the phone that
the airline will book his baggage straight through to New York,
knowing that citing such assurance later to a desk clerk at the
Milan airport, where his baggage has *not* been checked
through, will have about as much weight as it did to insist,
when as a child he was made the victim of grown-ups' peremp-
tory rule changes, "But you *said* . . . "

This was after I'd spent a half hour waiting for my bags to
thump onto the carousel and then wrestled them upstairs to

the gate for New York, where a line of passengers shuffled forward beneath the high ceilings, crisscrossing other lines bound for Prague or Cairo or Miami. Incomprehensible announcements in many languages buffeted us. I tried cutting ahead; a guard yelled at me. "I'm supposed to be on that flight," I told him. He shrugged. The shrug was a way of distancing himself from his own authority, of disguising "I don't want to help you" as "It can't be helped." In that way, it was very Italian. F. had already boarded. An attendant let me call her from the counter. We exchanged despairing good-byes. Who knew how long I'd be stranded here? Abruptly, her tone lightened. "Gattino's doing really well," she told me. "He hasn't made a peep." I may have asked her if he missed me, and she may have sworn, in a voice rich with theatrical insincerity, that he did. I remember laughing, and I remember the attendant looking at me with what, given the circumstances, was probably surprise.

I spent the next hour or two waiting in front of various counters, wobbling between abjection and fury. (Under similar conditions, Italians went straight to fury: F. told me that on the flight over, she and her fellow passengers had been marooned for hours at this same airport, where the Italian men had expressed their displeasure by racing up and down the stairs, shouting oaths, and tearing off their suit jackets and flinging them to the floor.) Getting home less than three days later cost me another $800. Actually, if you count the price of the charmless airport hotel where I spent the night and ate the only bad meal I ever had in Italy, it cost me more.

A limitation of the lyric mode is that it typically enacts only one big feeling at a time, or sometimes a sequence of feelings like the rooms in a museum through which the visitor passes, looking first at the Cimabues, then the Giottos, the Botticellis, the Ghirlandaios, a Michelangelo displayed behind bullet-proof glass. Somewhere there may be some early Masaccios. This limitation may be a natural consequence of the immense, transfixing energy those feelings possess, whether in themselves or through the amplification of poetic language. And it's true that looking back, the lover is likely to remember his feelings the same way. Each filled him so completely that to add even a dropperful of another emotion would have burst his heart. For this reason, even the most despairing lyric conveys a kind of joy. Few joys are greater than the joy of feeling one thing completely, to the utter exclusion of anything else. It's probably not too different from what the angels feel as they sing beneath the dome of heaven, only the angels feel it for eternity.

A husband rarely has the luxury of feeling one thing completely. He's too busy checking the entries in the Michelin guide and copying road directions from his laptop onto a piece of paper so his wife can read them to him as he drives instead of fumbling with his stupid BlackBerry. Much of the time, he doesn't know what he feels at all. And some of the feelings that impinge on his consciousness are so devoid of lyricism, so tepid and dishwater gray, that no poem could be written about them unless it were by Philip Larkin. The shame of hearing a dozen drivers backed up at the exit of a parking garage sound their horns at him—of *feeling* the horns' blast like a blow between his shoulder blades—as he walks over to the *cassa* to purchase a new ticket, a shame compounded by the peevish thought that they could get out of here quicker if his wife would at least offer to pay the cashier so he could move the car as soon as the gate was raised. But she says her Italian isn't good enough, and wouldn't it be cowardly to subject her to the brays of the fuming motorists behind them, though maybe they wouldn't honk like that at a woman? No, they would.

The impatience that mars his pity as he watches her weeping over what is, after all, just a cat. Even as he feels this, he understands that "after all" and "just a cat" are phrases he will have to keep secret from her until the day he dies.

The white-knuckled anger of circling endlessly around the Aventine in his flimsy Lancia, crossing and recrossing the Ponte Sublicio or is it the Ponte Testaccio? Impossible to tell, since the traffic moves quickly and the streets don't have proper signs with their names on them, only stone plaques on the sides of buildings that might be legible to somebody on horseback, if the streets were better lit, which they aren't. With each circuit, he becomes more angry—*who built this fucking city?*—but also more afraid, because it seems they'll never find the street they're looking for, just keep whipping around and around until they run out of gas or get rear-ended by one of the cars behind them: by Italian standards, he's driving like somebody's *nonno.*

But his wife wants him to slow down. In the glow of the headlights, her skin is ashen, and the small vein above one eye is throbbing. "Don't you know where we are?" she pleads. Through clenched teeth, he says, "In principle." Her voice gets higher. She's tired; she's hungry; she's dehydrated. They should never have driven into Rome. He says she's right and imagines wrenching open the passenger door and kicking her into the street. She begins to whimper, a horrible sound. It's this that makes him pull over to a curb. "Okay," he says, "we'll stop. Look, look, I'm stopping." There is a space—he doesn't know if it's legal, but fuck it, let the fucking *polizia* give him a fucking ticket. He tells her to get out. She looks at him in fright. Can she have guessed what was in his mind a few moments ago? He makes his voice softer. "Let's get out and find something to drink." He takes her by the hand and leads her to a little grocery store whose lights cast a bluish-white trapezoid onto the sidewalk. Stepping inside, he has the momentary illusion that they've entered a bodega in his old neighborhood in the city, a place where you could buy a bag of plantain chips and a Diet Coke: the Diet Coke in Italy is terrible. He asks for a bottle of water and hands it to her. "Drink," he says. She protests. They don't know where they are. "Shut up," he says, but he says it gently. "Just drink." It's only watching her tilt her head back and take long, grateful swallows from the upended bottle—a creaturely gratitude that isn't directed at him but at the water itself—that he remembers he loves her.

We don't think of cats as beings that feel two things at once, but this is one explanation—as far as I know, only an anecdotal one—for why they sometimes lash their tails. And when Bitey was dying, F. noticed that Suki, who usually was just cranky, seemed both angry and sad. For most of the night, she remained in the narrow hallway outside the bathroom where my cat sat listlessly in the tub. Her expression was unmistakably a glare. But once F. pointed out that her eyes were filled with liquid. The liquid was clear and bright, and it ran down the gray tabby's cheeks, and I don't think it's too great a stretch to call it tears. They may or may not have been tears of grief.

~~~

By the time New York appeared below us, it was dark. Most of my memories of landing there take place at night, though when I'd come back from Italy the year before, it was afternoon. That may be part of why it felt so anticlimactic. On October 2, 2008, my plane landed at night, the voluptuous night of New York in autumn, violet as ink and lit from beneath by the radiance of its traffic, not just the vehicular kind but the traffic of money and its shape-shifting surrogates—collateralized debt obligations, credit default swaps—the traffic of power, the traffic of beauty, the traffic of appetite, of talent, of sex. Everything was moving; every lighted window signaled others. And in darkened offices, machines spoke to other machines thousands of miles away in a language of pulses, clicks, and blinking lights. An immense conversation was taking place below, and the aircraft circled it the way a newcomer circles the fringes of a party, a party where his welcome is uncertain; he sees nobody there he knows.

A wing dipped, then sliced across the face of the moon. Slowly, we dropped.

~~~

We didn't get a parking ticket that evening in Rome, but ironically, I got one later, in Arezzo. I'm speaking figuratively. There was no physical ticket, and I had no idea I'd done anything wrong until some months after my return to the United States, when I received a citation from the Polizia Autostradale of the Region of Tuscany charging me with illegal parking and demanding €100. I tore it up. A while later, I got a second citation in which the fine was raised to €150. This time I wrote back, asking (in English) for some evidence of the violation. None was given me. Instead, the citations kept coming and the fine kept rising until it reached €250. At that point, I took down my Italian dictionary and wrote back:

Egregi signori,

Ho ricevuto la vostra domanda di pagamento per parcheggio illegale nel commune di Arezzo la notte del 28 luglio 2007. Purtroppo, devo rifiutare di pagare quest' ammenda eccessiva e ingiusta. Non c'era nessun segno o avertenza riguardo al fatto che era vietato parcheggiare nel posto in questione. Nessuno ha lasciato qualche tipo di avviso sul parabrezza della mia macchina. Inoltre, sono disoccupato e pieno di debiti, e la ultima bolletta che pagherò è una di quasi quattrocento dollari data per una infrazione che non ho mai commesso, e certo non per colpa mia.

Distinti saluti,

_____.

There were no further requests.

To be honest, this is only an approximation of my original letter, which I didn't keep. At the time, I figured that either it would achieve its purpose or it wouldn't, and if it didn't, I would just keep stonewalling until the Polizia Autostradale got tired of dunning me. Maybe it was naive to assume they wouldn't hit on the expedient of putting a lien on my bank account, but then again, if they could do that, Italy wouldn't be going bankrupt, would it? The Italian of the original was almost certainly worse, since I dashed it off in a rage, and I doubt it included the word *parabrezzo*, "windshield." Still, I was pleased with myself for having pulled off a letter of this kind in a foreign language, and I would have shown it to F. if I hadn't been afraid of reminding her of Gattino. By then he was gone and, I'm pretty sure, dead.

8

I DON'T REMEMBER CHECKING A BAG—I DON'T KNOW why I would have checked one for a short trip—but I know I was in baggage claim when I played back Bruno's message. I have a clear memory of standing by a brushed-steel conveyer belt with my phone wedged against my ear and hearing his voice for the first time in almost a week; it sounded hesitant and apologetic. I thought it would be more bad news. He said something about Biscuit, but the next words were obscured by a thudding cascade of luggage that might have been the commotion of my heart. Is that what Ruskin meant by the pathetic fallacy? I had to play back the message to hear Bruno say he'd spotted Biscuit in the yard and almost succeeded in putting her back inside. He'd picked her up (only later would I appreciate the screwing up of will that must have demanded of him), but she'd scratched him (I could hear his incredulity and hurt) and gotten away. He was sorry. When had this happened? I kept playing the message back, but he never said. At the moment it didn't matter; I was too happy. I called him; it went straight to voicemail. For once, I wasn't irritated. I spoke in the praising tones one uses with very young children. How great was it that he'd seen Biscuit! He probably shouldn't have tried picking her up, but his intention had been good, and at least we knew she was still alive and near the house, right? That was really great. Could he tell me just when this had happened? Oh, and I was in New York; I'd just landed. I'd probably be up there in a couple hours. No need for him to wait up for me, but if he didn't mind, could he leave the light in the driveway on?

~ ~ ~

By the time I got home from Milan, F. had installed Gattino in a spare room on the side of the house. It had its own entrance, so the other cats didn't yet seem to be aware of his presence. But Gattino knew we were somewhere without him. In the morning he raced to greet us at the door, and even if F. or I spent most of the day in the room with him, he was always crestfallen when we left, or so it seemed to me from the way he'd try to leave with us and, when nudged back, would sit down heavily and look up at us with his one eye. He'd gotten used to sleeping with us.

Maybe this was what F. meant when she said that love—the human kind—is too big and complex a feeling for a cat. It may also be too perverse, since it involves treating a self-sufficient adult animal as an infant, *our* infant, and in turn encourages the animal to behave as if it were one. Like every other creature, a cat in the wild will know the discomfort of wanting and not getting. It will know cold and hunger: kittens are supposed to have separate cries for each. A domesticated cat will be held against its will (witness the indignant squeak Biscuit would make when you picked her up); it will be shooed off dining tables and kitchen counters, though not F's and mine, and have alluring objects like electrical cords snatched away from it. But in its natural state, a cat is mostly a solitary being. Its couplings are brief and scored to a soundtrack of screeches. Males are known to kill their young. It is a stranger to the pain of being separated from what it loves because it's a stranger to love, or love is strange to it. Now we had introduced a cat to that foreign thing, that xenograft, and maybe to a new kind of pain. It was too early to tell.

That summer was one of the last times Wilfredo stayed with us. It was a bad visit, which was probably more our fault than his. We were in the middle of packing, and so everything we did with him, we did only dutifully. I'm sure he picked up on that; it may explain why he regressed. One morning in the kitchen, he told F. he wanted her to feed him his cereal. He opened his mouth expectantly, importunately, like a baby bird. We could see the remnants of his last few bites caked between his teeth. He was almost as tall as I was and had heavy breasts that embarrassed him so much he refused to take off his T-shirt when we took him swimming. F. told him not to be gross, though really, how could you expect an eleven-year-old boy not to be gross? It would be expecting him to forego the highest expression of who he was, or, really, *what* he was, the apotheosis of his boy's smeary, spewing, burping, farting nature.

That was the summer he threatened to cut off my nuts. To put it in context, he made the threat after he'd learned we were planning to have Gattino neutered and immediately after he'd learned what neutering involved. I wouldn't be surprised if he unconsciously equated the cat with himself: they were two young males with Latino names and some physical habits that F. and I considered repulsive. We knew it was time to have Gattino neutered because when excited, he'd begun to give off a rank smell, a jet of pure male horniness and aggression.

Every year before this, we'd taken Wilfredo home on the train, but this time we decided to drive to the city. I'm not sure why. F. was in a terrible mood. She was relieved Wilfredo was leaving, but she felt guilty about it. And for the first time, she admitted to being disappointed in him. She'd dreamed that through us he'd learn to Rollerblade and ride a bike and act in plays and write a book report he could get a passing grade on, and none of that had happened. Or rather, he'd learned to do some of those things, but as soon as he did, he lost interest in them, as if all along they'd only been items on a list that had to be checked off to get us off his back. In that way, he was as perfunctory as we were. With F.'s tutoring, he wrote an excellent report on *The Call of the Wild.* But I wasn't terribly surprised later when I learned that he never handed it in. He'd written it: what more did we want?

On the drive to the city, F. sat beside me and talked about how worthless love was. How it arose out of the sensible needs of the organism but, at least in human organisms, so often morphed into something twisted and self-defeating. She wasn't even sure there was such a thing as love. Abruptly, something small and soft bounced off her head and landed on the seat between us. It was a stuffed animal that Wilfredo had tossed at her from the backseat. He'd won it at the county fair the day before. "Here," he said, in the helpful if slightly condescending tone of someone who's found something you've been going wild looking for. "What do you call that?"

In time, Biscuit and the other cats began to loiter outside the spare room and peer in at its windows. One morning I came out to find that Gattino had succeeded in pushing out a screen and was sitting on the wet grass, looking quizzically about him. A few yards away, Zuni watched him with moon eyes, trying to decide whether to approach or run for her life. Did he have any clue that he was 5,000 miles from the place where a human being had first lifted him off the ground? Did the grass smell different from the grass that had grown in his farmyard? Were there different bugs crawling in it? I scooped him up and put him back inside, feeling him buckle and squirm, all sinew and short, coarse fur. He was getting to be a strong little cat.

I don't remember if we introduced him to the others before the move. It would have been a bad idea, given the disorder of the house, the stacks of boxes and the stacks of books and dishes waiting to be boxed in their turn, the doors left open, the limitless, limitless opportunities for loss or breakage. But if you picture one of those wall calendars that are used to show the passage of time in old movies, each page of the calendar of that summer—and, really, of the preceding spring—would have the words "Bad Idea" scrawled across it, and when that page was torn away, underneath there would be another page that said the same thing: "Bad Idea." It was a bad idea to have Wilfredo visit us before the move. It was a bad idea not to look inside the oven in the empty house we were about to move into. It was a bad idea not to run the washing machine. It was a bad idea to take the landlord's word that heat would run $200 to $300 a month in winter and not ask to see some heating bills. It was a bad idea to trust him to remove the bags of old clothes and toiletries and ordinary garbage, though, thankfully not organic garbage—it didn't smell—that had been left in the closets. When F. asked about the garbage, I said of course Rudy would take it away; we'd been to his and his wife's Christmas parties. That was how F. had fallen in love with the house in the first place, though it was probably a bad idea to fall in love with a house she'd only seen lit by candles and Christmas tree lights, the same way it's inadvisable to fall in love with some-one you've only seen in dimly lit restaurant booths or in the roseate glow of a hotel room's bedside lamp.

It was a bad idea not to ask F. if she wanted to think twice about moving to the new house. It was a bad idea to take her at her word when she said she didn't. It was probably ill-advised, when she expressed misgivings about things like the garbage in the closets, to ask (or, according to F., yell), "Well, what do you want to do then? You want to just cancel? Fine, then *you* find us a place to live."

It was a bad idea to hire a mover who had only recently fin-ished withdrawing from the drugs he'd gotten hooked on after injuring his back some months earlier, and when he told us he had a truck and trailer, it was foolish not to find out exactly what he meant by a truck and trailer: I was thinking of the fourteen-footer I'd rented eight years before. But the mover's truck turned out to be a pickup and his trailer one of those lattice-sided ones, like a playpen on wheels, that you use to transport a ride mower, and F.'s and my possessions made up not one load, but more than a dozen, not counting the additional loads we stuffed into our car. The move ended up taking two whole days—three, if you count the cleanup.

Late the first night, at around the time we were bringing up items from the basement, I decided to bury the ashes of my old tomcat. They were in the pantry, inside the handsome wooden box in which the vet had returned them after I'd had the poor guy put down the year before, a dazed skeleton who crapped in the tub and screamed to be fed a dozen times a day. The box had been included in the price of a premium cremation. I half expected F. to argue. It was late; Ching had been my cat, not hers, and she'd resented him for the way he'd joined Bitey in tormenting poor Tina, like a big oaf of a kid who allies himself with the class bully. But she'd been kind to him during his long decline, often kinder than I was, and she didn't protest. It was too dark to bury him in the yard behind the house; that was where we'd interred Bitey's ashes and Suki's body, after she'd died three years before at the age of nineteen. By the light from the porch lamp, I started digging a hole beneath the maple on the front lawn, where he'd loved to lie. A proper grave for a cat, or for the ashes of one, would be about a foot square and three feet deep. It had been a dry summer, the earth was hard, and once I broke its surface, I encountered a web of roots that ran through the soil like rebar through concrete. I started one hole after another, moving farther and farther out until I was almost in the driveway, and every time I was thwarted by the same unyielding earth and roots that twanged beneath the shovel blade. From the car, F. called, "What's wrong?" In my memory, it was "For God's sake, what's wrong?" and who could blame her, given that it was after eleven and I was cursing loudly across the street from houses where children slept? I told her to wait a minute. I said it again, and then several times more. I felt her impatience like the ticking of a bomb. But maybe what I was feeling was just the shame of fucking up another move, committing an entire household to a vehicle suitable for hauling sacks of horseshit. It was only by digging just at the foot of a tall, black hemlock like a tree in an Edward Gorey print that I was able to get down a foot, making what was less a hole in the ground than a notch. It was so dark here that F. had to come over and hold a flashlight so I could see where to pour the ashes. Even so, I ended up spilling a lot on the tree trunk and, I discovered later, on my jeans and work boots. "Good-bye, my sweet friend," I told the old tom. "Be at peace." But how could he be, when a portion of his substance was sprinkled on my clothing like the ash from a barbecue, to be rinsed off in the next wash?

In *Modern Painters*, the critic John Ruskin identifies three ranks of perception:

> The man who perceives rightly, because he does not feel, and to whom the primrose is very accurately the primrose, because he does not love it. Then, secondly, the man who perceives wrongly, because he feels, and to whom the primrose is anything else than a primrose: a star, or a sun, or a fairy's shield, or a forsaken maiden. And then, lastly,

there is the man who perceives rightly in spite of his feelings, and to whom the primrose is for ever nothing else
than itself—a little flower apprehended in the very plain
and leafy fact of it, whatever and how many soever the
associations and passions may be that crowd around it.

I'm not that familiar with Ruskin's work, but his categories
seem sensible to me. This is not an adjective I'd associate with
him, given the vinous extravagance of his prose and the weird-
ness of his personal life. In 1848, at the relatively advanced age
of twenty-nine, Ruskin married Effie Gray. She was nineteen.
Both of them were virgins.

He had been infatuated with her since meeting her two
years before. The letters he wrote her during that time throb
with longing, but also with what is pretty clearly sexual dread:

You are like a sweet forest of pleasant glades and whisper-
ing branches—where people wander on and on in its playing shadows they know not how far—and when they come
near the centre of it, it is all cold and impenetrable. . . .
You are like the bright—soft—swelling—lovely fields of a
high glacier covered with fresh morning snow—which is
lovely to the eye—and soft and winning on the foot—but
beneath, there are winding clefts and dark places in its
cold—cold ice—where men fall and rise not again.

Following the wedding ceremony at the home of the
bride's parents, the couple traveled by carriage to Blair Atholl
in the Scottish highlands, where they were to spend the night.

What happened in the bedroom was later recorded by Ruskin's lawyer, who made notes of what his client told him when he was contesting the annulment of his marriage. John and Effie changed into their nightclothes. He lifted her dress from her shoulders. He looked at her. Then he lowered her garment, and after a chaste embrace, they went to bed and slept uneventfully through the night. So they would sleep for the rest of their married life. He told her that he was against having children, who would interfere with his work and make it impossible for her to keep him company when he traveled abroad. There is no evidence as to whether Effie proposed another method of birth control, or knew of one. When she protested that chastity was unnatural, John reminded her that the saints had been celibate. And so she acquiesced, and the Ruskins' marriage remained unconsummated until 1854, when she left him and filed for annulment, provoking a scandal almost as great as those that accompanied the later breakups of Prince Charles and Diana Spencer or John and Elizabeth Edwards. A significant difference was that public outrage fell on the reluctant—I suppose now you would say "withholding"—husband who had refused to give the wife her debitum. According to the notes taken by Ruskin's lawyer, John told him that when he removed Effie's dress, he was disappointed. Her body was not what he had imagined women's bodies as being like. It was, he said, "not formed to excite passion." In a letter to her parents, Effie put it less circumspectly: "The reason he did not make me his Wife was because he was disgusted with my person."

This is not at odds with Ruskin's prior experience of female bodies, which was probably limited to the idealized forms of classical statuary, or to the fact that at the age of forty he would fall in love with a ten-year-old girl.

Ruskin admired Masaccio, especially his rendering of landscapes, but I find no reference in his writings to *The Expulsion from the Garden of Eden.* It would be interesting to know what he thought of the figure of Eve. Like other female images the critic was familiar with, Masaccio's Eve has no pubic hair (one of Ruskin's biographers speculates that it was this feature of Effie's anatomy that caused him to drop her nightdress). Unlike them, she has the sexual characteristics of a mature woman. He might have viewed the painting as an allegory of his own wedding night: the man shielding his face in horror, the woman covering her swelling fields and winding cleft in shame. In this, he would have been hew-

Masaccio, *The Expulsion of Adam and Eve from The Garden of Eden* (1426–1428), Cappella Brancacci, Santa Maria del Carmine. Courtesy of the Granger Collection.

ing to the ancient scheme that classifies the genders as subject and object, viewer and viewed, knower and known.

But in the story of the Fall, both Adam and Eve are active seekers of knowledge, Eve even more than Adam. Both are punished for knowing something they're not supposed to know. It may be the narcotic sweetness of a fruit whose name has been lost to us; it may be the shudder of concupiscence; it may be good and evil, those words that meant nothing until suddenly they meant everything. Just for a moment, Genesis confers on the sexes an odd equality, which it then takes away when Adam is given dominion over his wife. At the same time, both Adam and Eve are objects of knowledge, members of the class of the known. It's God who knows them, and it's his gaze they try to hide from—at first so effectively that he calls out to them, "Where are you?" (Gen. 3:9). That a being who is supposed to be all seeing and all knowing must call, "Where are you?" to his creations is one of the story's most resistant mysteries, and one of its most poignant. To me, God's call is very poignant. It's like a parent's call to missing children. That, of course, is how many Christians read it, saying of the first couple not that they fell but that they strayed.

At once knower and known, the man and the woman are like people who look in a mirror for the first time and see themselves looking back. "And the eyes of them both were opened, and they knew that they [were] naked." (Gen. 3:7). To understand the vast gulf between the Greek and Hebrew worldviews, consider that Narcissus falls in love with his reflection and Adam and Eve recoil from theirs. But, then, they don't see themselves in a pond, but in each other's eyes. The eyeball is convex, and a convex mirror gives a distorted reflection. Maybe the first forbidden knowledge was how weak and uncomely they were in their nakedness, he with his drooping finger of prick and she with her lopsided tits and goosefleshed

bum. Their eyes were as merciless as teenagers'. And perhaps
their nakedness was more than a condition of the body, and
what they saw were the wens and stretch marks of each other's
characters. Up until this moment, they hadn't even *had* characters, being only another species of animal; it's well known that
no animal has a character until it is claimed by a human being.
But now they had them. How lacking those characters were,
how stunted and deficient! The man was easygoing, slothful,
weak willed. The woman was greedy and shrill. And, really, she
wasn't bright either. She'd believed what a snake had told her.
He saw her and was disgusted with her person. She looked at
him and thought, "He is not formed to excite passion."

I'd had the house painted before we moved in, so it looked
cleaner. F.'s attic study was now trimmed in Mediterranean
blue. But the closets were still filled with the landlord's trash.
The stove was broken and had a mouse nest inside it, and
when we turned on the washing machine, it vomited gallons of
hot water onto the floor of the barn. I got Rudy to buy a new
stove and fix the washer, but by then F. had decided he was our
enemy. The garbage might have been left as a taunt for her, as if
Rudy had conferred with the vile old Broadway eminence
who'd once accused her of dining on it. "Why don't you say
something to him?" she'd reproach me. It bothered her that I
didn't think he was our enemy. I'd remind her that I *had* said
something; that was how we'd gotten the new stove. But whatever I'd said, I'd said mildly, making a joke out of what, even in
the city, where landlords are permitted by law to seize your internal organs if you're late paying the rent, would have been

grounds for breaking the lease. I wanted Rudy to like me. Even now I'm embarrassed to admit it.

At least the cats enjoyed the house. It had been built in the 1850s—by a black freedman, according to Rudy, who prided himself on knowing the history of the valley—and then expanded with additions at either end, but it still had a long central aisle that was perfect for cats to scramble noisily up and down, especially late at night. Biscuit quickly staked a claim to the kitchen island. And all the cats liked roaming in the garden, with its lilac and apple trees, its beds of hosta, peonies, and day lilies in whose foliage small creatures nested, waiting to be killed. Out back there was a burrow occupied by a groundhog that looked like it must weigh thirty pounds. Once I saw it running—could Biscuit have had the nerve to chase it?—and thought I could feel the earth shake. Of all the cats, it was Gattino who seemed to be having the best time. He'd scuttle fearlessly up the smooth trunk of the horse chestnut that grew in the front yard and out onto branches fifteen feet above the ground, from where he surveyed the garden with a seigneurial air. "Gattini!" F. would trill to him, and he'd streak back down, half climbing, half leaping, and let her take him in her arms. I've always thought that a test of a cat's personality is whether it enjoys this and, if not, how long it will put up with it. Bitey resisted being picked up with every claw and fang. Biscuit protested at first but could be jollied into lying still for ten seconds or so. Gattino liked it. You could carry him around like a baby.

For the most part, he got along with the other cats. It helped that he was still young. He and Biscuit used to wage mock battles, darting and rearing, he on his long legs and she on her short ones. But by now she was a full-grown cat, almost middle-aged. She lacked Gattino's energy and appetite for play, and there were times you could see her wearying of being pounced on when she was trying to get a drink of water or having him dive at her food bowl, not to eat but to bat bits of kibble around the floor. She'd done the same when she was a kitten, but she had put away kittenish things and knew not to play with her food any more. If I were nearby, I'd clap my hands to make him leave her alone. Once I blocked him roughly with my foot and locked him in my bedroom until Biscuit could finish eating. When I let him out fifteen minutes later, his high spirits were intact and he appeared to bear me no ill will, but I find it significant that I didn't tell F. about it.

One moment from that autumn stays with me. I was in the living room, listening to a CD I'd put on the stereo, Joni Mitchell's *Ladies of the Canyon*. I hadn't listened to it in years and was a little surprised to realize I had it, or any of her albums, on CD. She seems so much an artist of vinyl; her voice, which you remember for its birdlike high notes but which has an unexpected deep end, needs physical grooves to rise out of, and only records have those. "Woodstock" came on, and suddenly my eyes were filled with tears. I walked into the kitchen. I didn't want the song to stop, but I needed distance from it. "What's wrong?" F. asked. I gestured helplessly at the speakers. "I don't know. It's beautiful, it's sad." And then, "I want to get back to the garden." I meant to say it jokingly, but my voice broke. F. started crying. "I do too." We held each other.

Early that November, I spent a day working in the city. When I
came back that night, Gattino was gone. F. had gone out to visit
some friends; the cats had been in the garden. She'd considered
calling him in, but she would only be away a little while, and it
was still light. When she returned, the other cats were waiting by
the back door. Gattino was nowhere in sight. That had been five
hours ago. I told her it was too early to worry. The cats often
stayed out late. We went out into the yard and called his name
under the moon. I thought the problem might be that he hadn't
heard F.—her voice is soft—and I half expected him to come
running in response to my manly bellow, hungry, his eye alight.
It would be another thing I fixed, like F.'s laptop or the furnace
that stopped putting out heat until I pushed its red reset button,
which I knew how to do because of the instructions printed underneath. Of course I was forgetting the time I'd tried bleeding
the radiator in my old loft. "GATTINO!" I yelled. "GATTINO!" My
voice hung in the chill air. He didn't come.

The next day I called his name up and down the road that
ran behind our house. It belonged to the college next door and
filed past dormitories, woods, and a theater before emptying at
length into a parking lot. Once, back in the summer, when I
was clearing ailanthus from the garden, I'd looked up and seen
a young woman walking down that road, bare breasted and
martially erect, then turn and vanish into the dorm behind us.
I imagine she was doing it on a dare. The few cars that passed
now were traveling slowly, and I was reassured by the thought
that if Gattino had wandered off this way, he was probably safe.
I don't remember if it was that night or the next that F. looked

across Avondale Road, which ran past our front door, and realized, with a start of sick fear, that neither of us had thought of searching in that direction. In the few months Gattino had been going out, we'd always shooed him back from Avondale because there was so much traffic there and it moved so fast. Many years before, not a hundred feet from the house, a car had struck and killed a little girl who was crossing on her way to nursery school. The school was now named after her.

We searched farther and farther from the house, along back roads and footpaths, in people's yards and in a sinister abandoned barn that was always ten degrees colder than it was outside, like a morgue. We put up posters. We stuffed flyers in mailboxes and taped them to the doors of the college dorms:

MISSING CAT

GATTINO IS A 6-MONTH-OLD, SLENDER GRAY MALE TABBY WITH DISTINCTIVE SPOTS AND STRIPES. HE'S BLIND IN HIS LEFT EYE. LAST SEEN TUESDAY, NOVEMBER 13, AT 5:00 PM, OUTSIDE HIS HOME ON AVONDALE ROAD.

IF YOU FIND HIM, PLEASE CONTACT HIS HEARTBROKEN OWNERS XXX-XXX-XXXX OR XXX-XXX-XXXX. HIS HEALTH IS DELICATE AND HE NEEDS MEDICAL ATTENTION.

At night we set traps and in the morning released the irate strays we found inside, each crouched beside an empty can of Friskies like a dragon guarding its hoard. Sometimes we speculated about how long it

must take the captives to get over their initial panic and start eating. It was F. who organized us. Her earlier vagueness might
have been a disguise that she had now cast off. But, really, she'd
gone through most of her life alone and unaided, with her head
down, applying herself to the business of survival. I'd just forgotten that. She had us call every animal shelter within fifty miles.
She posted Gattino's picture on animal-finder websites. She
consulted psychics. At first only F. did this, since she believes in
psychics, or half believes in them, but when one of them told
her that she was sensing Gattino near a body of moving water, it
was me who burned rubber to the creek a half mile away to pace
its banks with an open container of cat food. I came back day after day. It didn't matter what I believed. Once, I called a psychic
myself, though she described herself—kind of sniffily—as an
"animal communicator." She told me that Gattino was dead,
which I reported to F. She told me something else that I did not
report: that he was a reincarnation of F.'s father, who had come
back to show her how to "let go." I still think it was a good idea to
keep this to myself.

Most of the psychics told us our cat was dead. It was this
that made me trust them. Somebody who wanted to rip us off
would have told us that Gattino was alive and could be coaxed
back if we burned some candles and left $500 in a shopping
bag at the door of St. Sylvia's. I might have done that if somebody had told me to; I might have rolled in a pile of shit on our
front lawn. The one time I drew the line was when a half-liter-
ate stranger e-mailed F., having gotten her address from a shelter's website, and told her that his friend Samuel had found
Gattino and taken a fancy to him and brought him back with

him to Cameroon. All we had to do was wire him the price of a plane ticket, and he'd send him home. I don't remember whether we were supposed to pay for tickets for Samuel and Gattino or just Gattino, but "Cameroon" set off an alarm bell—so might "Belarus" or "Moldova" have done—and my misgivings were confirmed when we pasted it, along with the terms "Samuel" and "cat" into Google and found the outraged testimonies of people who had sent off the money and never seen their pets again.

In winter, we were still searching. Late at night we'd get a call from a security guard at the college who'd seen a one-eyed cat scrabbling in a dumpster. We'd throw coats on over our pajamas, drive fishtailing on the icy roads, and end up in a parking lot where a man in a down jacket shone his flashlight onto the snow. "He was just here." We'd stand there stricken. The guard would go back to his rounds, and we'd put out a can of cat food—we spent a fortune on cat food that year—and sit in the car with the lights off, hoping that if we waited long enough, Gattino, if it was Gattino, might return. One night I caught a glimpse of a small, thin creature slinking under a parked car. It might have been a cat; it might have been a fox or a stoat. At any other time, I would have been thrilled to spot a wild animal near college dorms where kids from the city were smoking dope and reading Heidegger. But all I wanted to see was our cat. I wanted to bring him to F. like a treasure. I opened the door and stepped out slowly into the cold. I barely broke the membrane between stillness and motion. Many, many minutes later, I reached the car where the creature had hidden. I shone my light beneath it, then dropped into a crouch to see better. My knees hurt. How had I gotten so old? There was no sign of a cat.

~~~

Outside the airport it was cold, and the city's garish carnival night was full of moving lights. Already I'd forgotten what it was like to be someplace that stayed bright after nightfall, apart from a two-block commercial strip where people went looking for action. No need to look for action here; it was everywhere, as in the interior of a spark chamber restlessly populated with subatomic fauna. Instead, you would have to look for stillness. You might not find it.

A bus took me downtown; a second one brought me across town to the railway station. I felt hopeful and eager. The feelings dimmed a little when I learned the next train wouldn't be leaving for more than an hour. I had the impulse to call F. to tell her not to come pick me up. While waiting, I sat in a deli staring at the immense orange faces of two politicians, a man and a woman, who were debating on TV. Never had I seen teeth so huge or eyes so lambent. The volume was turned down and I was sitting too far away to read the captioning, so I focused on the debaters' facial expressions. I might have been watching the actors in a silent movie, each holding up one or two big feelings for the audience to identify, approve of, and feel in turn. The man looked angry and, briefly, tearful. The woman, who for a pol was uncharacteristically attractive, even sexy, smiled and winked. The gesture—is a wink a gesture?— was so unexpected that I wondered if I was imagining it.

Who was she winking at? And was it a wink of flirtation or a signal that whatever she told her opponent shouldn't be taken too seriously, she was just gaming Mr. Man, and we, the audience, were in on it? Was that why we should vote for her?

~~~

During those months we were looking for Gattino, our lives continued in some distant version. We both worked or tried to work. I screwed up a proofreading job so grotesquely that I offered to reorganize the client's filing system for free, not because I hoped she'd rehire me—she would have had to be insane to do that—but because I wanted to feel less guilty. F. spent a lot of the time on the phone. She spoke with friends. She spoke with her sister, who she believed had psychic powers. She spoke with Wilfredo. She spoke with psychics. Sometimes she'd relay what the psychics had told her: Gattino had drunk some poisonous substance and died in agony. He'd died quietly, curling up into himself as if going to sleep. Once in a while, somebody told her that he was still alive.

These possibilities seemed equally valid to me. I switched from one to the other with barely a cognitive jolt, and at times I seemed to hold them all in mind at once. Looking back, I'm reminded of the thought experiment of Schrödinger's cat. The experiment is meant to illustrate the unpredictable and fundamentally unknowable behavior of particles on the quantum level. Any attempt to measure that behavior inevitably influences it. Until you look at the meter, you can't know if a deflected electron has veered to the right or the left. Before then, you might as well speak of two ghostly electrons streaking in

opposite directions or maybe a ghostly hybrid particle that moves in both directions at once. It's only when you do the measurement that one of those phantoms evaporates and the other solidifies into a "real" particle occupying an identifiable point in space.

The physicist Erwin Schrödinger translated this paradox to the macro level. He proposed a scenario in which a cat is placed inside a steel chamber that also contains a tiny bit of a radioactive substance hooked up to a Geiger counter and a vial of cyanide. In the course of an hour, there's a 50 percent probability that an atom of the isotope will decay. If it does, it sets off the Geiger counter, which releases a hammer that shatters the vial of cyanide and kills kitty. If the particle doesn't decay, the cat remains alive. Schrödinger explained that one could visualize the system as "having in it the living and the dead cat (pardon the expression) mixed or smeared out in equal parts."

As the diagram above suggests, the cat remains in this smeared, blurred state, equally alive and equally dead, until such time as an observer peers inside the chamber. The observer's eye is what breaks the spell of indeterminacy. Perhaps our cat had become such a ghostly hybrid, not in a sealed box but in the wide world. Only when someone observed him would he solidify into life or death. For the observation to be reliable, however, it would have to be performed by someone who recognized Gattino, not as a generic cat searching for food in the cold and dark but as himself: this cat and no other. I suppose that means he would have to be observed by someone who loved him.

We were both sad, but F.'s grief was of a different order than mine. It admitted no other feeling. In my memory, she is always gazing out the window with sunken eyes. She is always walking out of the house with a sheaf of flyers that she leaves in the same mailboxes where she left some the month before, like a faithful mourner leaving flowers at a grave. My grief was more porous. At times I had the thought that we were making a huge deal about what was, after all, just a cat. I didn't tell F. about this thought, which, even as I had it, felt petty, less indicative of moral discernment than of irritation at lost comforts. Maybe it was also about jealousy, though what could be more pathetic than a live man being jealous of a dead cat, or of a live cat and a dead one smeared out in equal parts? Maybe I wasn't jealous so much as envious of the single-mindedness of my wife's sorrow. Its purity was lyrical, a moment of loss extending to the farthest horizon. I could only grieve like a husband, pausing to call the oil company to schedule a delivery. It was winter, after all, and very cold, and when Rudy had told us that the heat would only cost $300 a month, he'd been full of shit.

On one of the first nights after Gattino's disappearance, F. told me that she'd heard a voice in her head saying, "I'm scared." Some time after that, the voice had returned. Now it said, "I'm lonely." Late one afternoon about two months later, she told me she'd heard the voice again. It said, "I'm dying," and then "good-bye." When she told me this, I let out a groan. I sank to the floor. She'd looked into the chamber and shown me what was inside. We went into her bedroom and lay down together, holding each other, but some part of her felt far away. Maybe it was with Gattino. In retrospect, I can't say how much of my grief was for our cat and how much was for F. So much of what I'd done during those months I'd done for her. It hadn't helped. And, of course, much of that grief was probably for myself, and I clung to F. with what James Salter calls "the simple greed that makes one cling to a woman."

That is from *Light Years*. A man's wife has just walked out of the house in which they spent their marriage, and in that moment he is parted not just from her but from everything that had been his life. "A fatal space had opened, like that between a liner and the dock which is suddenly too wide to leap; everything is still present, visible, but it cannot be regained."

The other cats seemed unaffected by Gattino's disappearance, almost oblivious to it. Maybe Biscuit was relieved not to have him pestering her any more. In the mornings, she ate with serene concentration, chewing and swallowing, chewing and swallowing, not stopping until her dish was empty. F. said that when she'd come home that afternoon to find all the cats but Gattino waiting by the back door, Biscuit had looked especially happy.

When I think back to the time F. and I got teary eyed listening to "Woodstock," I realize I'm not sure if it was before or after we lost our cat. I remember that it was a warm day, but that could have been soon after we moved in or the following spring. You can see what a difference that makes.

9

AFTER GATTINO WAS GONE, THE HOUSE, WHICH BEFORE had only irritated F., became hateful to her. We kept finding new things wrong with it. Ice and snow built up in a valley on the roof and, on melting, leaked into an interior wall so that the new paint ballooned in watery blisters like the marks of some loathsome skin disease. We discovered that the toilet was sinking into the bathroom floor—slowly, but with the threat that one day, when somebody sat down too heavily, it would plummet into the basement. I called Rudy to complain; he came over and made what repairs he could, but his presence made F. angrier. She'd stalk past him, tight-lipped, and lock herself in her room; then she'd be angry at me for talking to him. I'd be angry back.

"What do you want?" It seems to be the question I asked her more than any other. Only now does it occur to me what an odd question it is: F. and I had been together ten years, and you'd think that after all that time, I wouldn't have to ask. "Do you want to move? We don't have the money to move." It was half true: I didn't have the money. Perhaps I asked her if she wanted to leave, though it seems to me that given the ambiguity of the wording, I would have been afraid to.

"I don't like being here," she'd say, and in my memory she'd be looking not at the house or at Avondale Road, with its heedless, gnashing traffic, but at me.

The well-known symbolism of houses: *The Professor's House, The House of the Seven Gables, Bleak House, A Doll's House,* which Nora had to leave, each a metonymy for the lives that hum and gutter inside them. Swann's house, where he lives with the deceitful Odette, whom he has made his wife now that he no longer loves her; the fashionable house of the Guermantes, where the duke humiliates the duchess in front of the dinner guests. The house of Charlus, who loves to be beaten; the house of the Verdurins, who love to climb; the house where Marcel imprisons Albertine, whom he thinks he loves. We speak of relationships, too, as contained spaces, sites of comfort or constriction. *I'm in a relationship. I want out of this marriage.* Really, I wasn't sure I wanted to stay in it either. We didn't even like the same kinds of food. Yet, at the same time, a small, shocked voice cried out inside me—*but you promised!* The cry of a child in a car racing past the Dairy Queen.

On some level, I understood that F.'s anger was part of her grief. It was anger at a world that had been emptied of the thing she loved. I belonged to that world. At least I was familiar and intermittently comforting, and I had some understanding of what she was feeling. Other people had none. One evening we had dinner with a writer I'd met through friends. In the course of the meal, it emerged that he'd once considered buying our house, back when it was vacant. He asked F. if she liked living in it. Astonishingly, she said nothing about the sinking toilet or the garbage left in the closets. She said only that the house had been spoiled for her by a trauma. Then she told the writer how we'd lost Gattino. The whole time, he looked at her as if waiting for more. At last he asked, "So that was your trauma, was it?" He was English, and he may have had the English distaste for promiscuous displays of feeling, especially the false kind Americans are prone to. F. and I share that distaste, or used to share it. I could have vouched that her feelings were real, that I had them too, but it would have made both of us seem pathetic.

Anyway, the question he was really asking wasn't about authenticity but appropriateness, which varies not only from culture to culture but from person to person. The writer's wife was holding their small daughter. She was about a year old and charming as most children are at that age, looking about her with eyes full of light, grabbing things that her parents either deftly took away or let her hold as down payments on the world of objects that would one day be hers. At the time they were thinking of buying our house, did they know that a child had been killed crossing the road outside it? And if they had known, would they have bought it anyway?

The death of a child is said to be the most terrible of all losses. It's one of the few our culture still pays deference to.

Part of that has to do with biology, the fact that our children are a part of ourselves, the tendrils we cast forward into the future. And then, of course, a child is so small and helpless, eager, clumsy, so guileless or possessed of a guile so primitive that it fools no one, which is why we find it endearing. Once we carried our children in our arms; we washed their faces for them. When it was time to cross the street, we held their hands. Even parents whose children are long grown up remember doing that; I can remember doing it for my friends' children when they were small. I remember doing it for Wilfredo. Farther down the scale of grief is the loss of a wife or husband, a brother or sister, and after that the death of parents, which is taken almost for granted, since we're supposed to outlive them. What's the standard number of personal days companies give employees for the death of a parent? One, two days?

Yet the Victorians reckoned the loss of a husband as more dire than that of a child, at least judging by their dress codes. Widows were supposed to wear black crepe and full veil for two years. The first year, they wore the veil hanging over the face; the second, they were allowed to pin it back. Bereaved parents wore deep mourning for one year, after which they could transition to lighter fabrics in black, white, or gray. Widowers only had to mourn for a year. It pays to remember that Victorian women were completely dependent on their husbands, and the death of children was far more common that it is today. Hence the photographs of deceased children that were part of the decor of so many homes of the period. Often, the children are posed on the deathbed.

Copyright Museum of Mourning Photography and Memorial Practice, Oak Park, Illinois.

Where on the grief scale do you place a lost cat?

Considering what had happened to Gattino, it would have made sense to keep the other cats indoors. It was winter, so they didn't want to go out much. Still, once or twice a day Biscuit would plant herself by the back door and, if you didn't open it, start meowing and then tearing out her fur. Was it a spontaneous upwelling of frustration or Machiavellian blackmail, and if it was blackmail, how did she know it would work? It always did. I'd open the door; she'd step outside and turn to look back at me. I can't say if the look was one of triumph or uncertainty; she may have wanted to make sure I wasn't going to yank her back inside. Some days she'd bound out into the snowy garden, raising a small white explosion with each leap. At other times she was deliberate. You could tell by her paw prints. She'd step with care between the drifts and around the brittle stalks of last year's flower beds. She'd pause to listen for the scrabbling of burrowing mice. She might inspect the perimeter of the groundhog burrow, but, wisely, she didn't go inside it. Sometimes she climbed the plastic children's slide that Rudy had bought for his son when he was little and took up a perch at its summit, from which she could look out at the white garden and the deer-eaten hedges that screened it from the road but would pose no obstacle to a cat that wanted to go out in pursuit of a scent or a flash of movement. Cats are cautious animals, but they are animals, and certain things summon them irresistibly. They don't even try to resist them. They just go.

Maybe F. and I were weak or lazy, unable to resist our cats any more than they could resist the sight of a rabbit hopping across the road. But when we talked about it, we agreed that going outside made them happy—not in the panting, theatrical manner of dogs but quietly, intently, with no need to proclaim their well-being to onlookers. Going out was how they fulfilled their nature, inasmuch as we have any sense of what that nature might be. Cats are the creatures that domesticated themselves. They chose to come to us, knowing that we were where the food was. Unlike dogs, they may never have understood they were doing us a service. We just didn't stop them from killing rats. Humans trained dogs to do what we wanted, though the argument can be made that they trained us. We allowed cats to do what they were already inclined to do. For a long time, people fed them only intermittently, believing they could get by on vermin. (In 1837, a French writer cautioned that "the cat who is not given food is feeble and malingering; as soon as he has bitten into a mouse, he lies down to rest and sleep; while well fed, he is wide awake and satisfies his natural taste in chasing all that belongs to the rat family.") And in contrast to the vigilance and rigor involved in house training a dog, a cat has only to be shown the litter box, though it falls to its owners to scoop out the turds. Our relationship with cats is about care and affection, but it is also in a very deep way about permission. We must let them be what they are. It's not as if we can stop them.

But one of our cats — the smallest and most vulnerable one, the one F. loved the most — had gone off and never come back. Maybe he'd gone off to fulfill his nature; maybe he'd died in one of the awful ways the psychics had laid out for us: convulsing from poison or broken in the jaws of a coyote or slowly freezing in the shadows of the wood. Before he died, he might have been hungry and afraid. He might have been lonely, a feeling he would never have known if humans hadn't taken him in and fed him on the bitter milk of their love. F. thought a cat would understand death, even a young cat like Gattino, and she pointed to the brisk way the cats she knew had dealt with one that was dying, sniffing it once, then turning away. But then she remembered her old gray tabby weeping on the night Bitey died: in memory, the liquid in her eyes had become tears.

To truly let the thing you love be what it is means surrendering it, perhaps even to death.

In the midst of this, I was going broke; it was one of the things we fought about. We fought more or less politely, without yelling, without even getting that angry, until one or the other of us left the room, ostensibly to do something. The other one didn't follow. That spring, I was offered a yearlong teaching job in North Carolina, and I took it. F. would stay up north with the cats; I'd send her money for rent and utilities. We'd visit each other when we could. When you factored in the second rent, I'd actually be losing money, but I couldn't afford not to go. I was losing money where I was, mired in my torpor, teaching one day a week and selling about one magazine article a year, and at least we'd have medical insurance. F. was afraid of being alone in the house. Briefly, she threatened to get a gun. I managed to talk her out of it. She's not good with tools or machines, and the likely outcome was that she'd shoot herself in the foot or plug Rudy some morning when he came over to chip ice from the roof. I could see her telling the cops she'd thought he was a prowler.

A temporary solution came when she was invited to a residency in Italy. I was happy for her but also envious, and I felt a little peeved at not even getting a proper chance to leave her. I wanted her to pine for me. Instead, shortly after I started teaching, my wife would be flying to Rome, then motoring up north to spend a month being plied with Prosecco, prosciutto, and figs under the cypress trees. I worried that it might make her sad to be so close to where she'd found Gattino. She said it wouldn't: nothing could make her sadder than she already was. She said it defiantly, as if I were the one who'd asked her, "So that's your trauma?" Eight months had passed since our cat had disappeared: she was still wearing the black veil, and she was wearing it over her face.

But who was going to care for the cats? I couldn't take them down to North Carolina with me; my landlords there were allergic, and, anyway, I could think of few things more distressing for a cat than to be driven twelve hours in a crate and then cooped up for a year in a house full of strange, unclawable furniture. I could think of few things more distressing for a person than to be the one who drove three of them. We had to get a cat-sitter, not a once-a-day drop by but someone who'd stay in the house. Bruno was the child of friends, a big, strapping kid, raised on the Lower East Side back when it was a habitation of schizophrenics and junkies. He'd gone to the college next door and was still hanging around the neighborhood the way a lot of its graduates did, knowing that never again would they find a place where they and their ideas were taken so seriously. I flew back from North Carolina to show him around the house, which he clearly loved and was prepared to spend quality time in. He didn't just come with suitcases but with keyboard instruments and a Mac G4 whose monitor was bigger than our TV set and what appeared to be a month's worth of fancy groceries. He wasn't put off when I told him to be careful sitting down on the pot. But he seemed leery of the cats. When I warned him that they might jump up on the table while he was eating and try to get at his food, his eyes widened in alarm.

"What am I supposed to do then?"

"You pick them up and put them down on the floor."

"They'll let me pick them up?"

I wanted to ask F. if she thought we were making a mistake, but by the time this conversation took place, she was on her way to Europe. Still, I e-mailed her what I told Bruno, figuring she'd appreciate it:

"I doubt they'll be in a position to stop you."

Once or twice a week, on a schedule we set up by e-mail, F. and I would Skype each other. In theory, it was more intimate than the phone, more like being together in the same place instead of calling out to each other from across an ocean. But really, it felt more remote. I couldn't walk around the house with the phone pressed to my ear, peeling a cucumber at the sink or portioning cat food into three dishes; I had to sit at my desk, as if I were working. My wife's face smiling uncertainly out of a letterbox on my laptop screen made me think of software. You clicked on the icon, and she came jerkily alive. She was so small, and the room behind her was such a generic room, veiled in shadow with a European light fixture on the ceiling. I'd ask her what the weather was like there. After a pause—I doubt I'd ever asked her about the weather the whole time we'd been together—she'd tell me. Then she'd ask me what it was like where I was. This was the future that had been foreseen for us when we were kids, by comic books and science fiction movies with F/X crude as a cardboard robot. We had arrived there, and nobody had told us. I don't remember what we talked about. We weren't nearly as expressive as we were in our e-mails, which were still full of gossip and humor and, sometimes, tenderness. The technology that made us present to each other was too intrusive, the lag between words and the moving lips that uttered them, the way her face kept freezing or shattering into a cascade of pixels. Never had I been so conscious of *seeing* another person. After a while, we just made faces at each other. It was more fun.

As further evidence of Skype's inadequacy, I was once using it to talk with my twin nieces in Chicago when they asked to see Biscuit. She was right nearby so I lifted her into my lap and held her up to the webcam, and while the girls squealed with pleasure (God knows why, since they had cats of their own, big fat ones twice the size of any of mine), Biscuit was uninterested. She didn't even sniff the screen the way she would a telephone that voices were coming out of. Stoically, she sat on my lap, squirming only a little. It was one more thing I was subjecting her to. You could chalk this up to a cat's poor depth of visual field or to the fact that the squeaking figures on the screen had no smell (only now does it occur to me that on video feed, the girls were about the size of mice). Or you can

ascribe it to an innate refinement of perception that allows a cat to distinguish between a being in the world—what Heidegger calls *Dasein*—and a being reconstituted in cyberspace and to ignore the one in cyberspace, which has nothing nice to give her.

Maybe what I felt when F. and I Skyped was the anxiety that arises from sensing the disjunction between those beings. Intellectually, yes, I understood that what I was seeing on the screen was in fact F., or the light that had bounced off her in her room in Italy and then been captured by a webcam, digitized, and transmitted over the Internet as packets of data, just as what I was hearing was a digital transcription of her actual voice. I didn't think it was a special effect, though within my lifetime we may reach the point where we can no longer tell an actual person on the screen from a complex animation of that person, maybe stitched together from the billions of digital photo and video and audio samples that have been taken of her in her life-time, the ones she posed for, the ones snatched on the sly by surveillance cameras in banks, airports, office buildings, and subway stations, not to mention the cameras that gaze impassively down on our streets, waiting for someone to bite into the vouchsafed fruit and look up with juice shining on her lips.

But the F. that I was seeing and talking with was a mediated F., an F. that had been mediated over and over. Between the image on my screen and the woman in a room in Umbria lay an uncounted number of operations, as if a gold coin of great worth had been changed into one currency after another by a series of invisible money changers, one of whom eventually gave me what he said was a sum equivalent to the value of the coin. I guess it was in dollars. But what were the transaction fees? At those moments when F.'s voice didn't sync with the movements of her lips, what was she really saying? When her lively, changeable features were replaced by a Mondrian schematic that might be the universal skeleton of digital beings, what expression was being hidden from me? On seeing her face appear on my screen, I felt the pleasure I always felt on seeing her after some time apart, but how much of that pleasure was borrowed from memory? And if my memory had been as limited or, say, as capricious as Biscuit's, would I have looked at F. with the same incomprehension, seeing only a tiny, smiling figure in a window the size of a credit card, with a piping voice that was almost familiar?

When we speak of love, we must speak not only of desire but delight. Desire doesn't last very long—typically, no more than three years. Delight doesn't always last longer than that, but it can. Studies have yet to identify its upward limit. Delight is not a condition of lack but of sufficiency, a plenty wholly independent of the circumstance of possession. You don't have to possess the object of love to delight in it, any more than you have to possess the sun to bake voluptuously in its warmth. You can revel in the object from afar, regardless of whether she loves you back or is even aware of you crouching in your blind, camouflaged in your cloak of reeds. Just watching her is enough. I don't desire Biscuit; I'm relieved to say I never have. But thinking of her, I visualize her busy gait, the purposeful mast of her tail, her trills and chirps of greeting. I recall the way she rubs her jowls against mine, the way she rolls onto her side and pumps her hind legs to tear the guts out of an imaginary enemy, and I'm filled with pleasure. A similar pleasure comes over me when I think of F. Her high, round forehead, which seen in profile—say, on those afternoons she used to walk down Astor Road beside me—looks as innocent and intrepid as Mighty Mouse's. Her silent, pop-eyed grimace of mock frustration. The little grunt with which she settles into herself as she gets ready for sleep. Her Midwestern reticence and her heedless blurtings. The look of undisguised appetite she casts at a stranger's entrée in a restaurant, as if at any moment she might reach over and help herself to a forkful of it.

These details seem to reflect something pure and unself-conscious in the object, the object as she is when she thinks no one is looking. When I see my cat or my wife, I seem to be seeing her as she truly is, free of all my wonderful, occluding ideas about her, including (in F.'s case but not Biscuit's) the wonderful, occluding idea of desire. There's a Zen koan that asks, What was your original face before you were born? Perhaps what I am delighting in are those unborn faces, the woman's, the cat's. And perhaps this pleasure, so generous and self-renewing, allows us to participate, even at a remove, in what God may have felt as he looked down at his creation and became lost in its splendor, maybe to such a degree that for a time he forgot that he created it, that it was his.

In the foregoing, of course, the words "see" and "seeing" are used figuratively as well as literally. It's possible to delight in the love object even when one cannot actually see her, as, for example, when one is separated from the object by time or distance. Under such circumstances, one must be content with the images afforded by other faculties. One must imagine the object as she might be. One must remember her as she was.

Bruno didn't return phone calls with the promptness one values in a cat-sitter. The first week he was at the house, I had to leave four or five messages before he called back to tell me—wearily—that the cats were fine. When we Skyped, I told F. I was beginning to think the kid was a lox. As if he'd overheard this and resolved to make a better impression, the next week he called me on a Monday evening, before I'd even begun to pester him. But when his name came up on my caller ID, I felt a twinge of unease, and the moment I heard his voice, my whole being constricted like a single great muscle in spasm.

10

THE HOUR PASSED; A DISPATCHER'S VOICE, BLURRED by tiredness and bad acoustics, issued its summons. I made my way to the gate and boarded the late train I had taken so many times with F., the two of us drowsy but excited after a night in the city and eager for bed. The black river scrolled past. The mountains on the other side were invisible now; I could only feel their dreaming weight. The Catskills aren't high as mountains go—geologically speaking, they aren't even proper mountains but an ancient plateau carved into relief by millions of years of water erosion—but they're some of the oldest in America. Their original sediments were laid down during the Devonian period, 350 million years ago.

Washington Irving calls them "fairy mountains," foreshadowing the enchantment that propels the plot of his most famous story. Rip Van Winkle may be the only character in American literature to have a bridge named after him. The

honor seems all the more anomalous because the story that
bears his name is so lightweight. A village loafer, fleeing his
scolding wife, wanders into the mountains, where he meets an
odd company of men who dress in antiquated clothing and
amuse themselves by playing ninepins. They ply Rip with
booze till he falls into a drunken sleep. When he awakens, he
creeps back home, nervous about what his wife will put him
through for having spent the night abroad. Instead, he discov-
ers that twenty years have passed. His wife and most of the
people he knew are dead, and the only Rip Van Winkle his
neighbors have heard of is his son, who has grown up to be a
great idler in his own right. Old Rip is taken in by his daughter
and lives to a happy old age. The end. Offhand, that doesn't
seem worth a bridge.

When I got off at my country station, I reflexively looked
around for our car. On nights F. came to pick me up, I always
loved the moment when I first saw its headlights shine at me
across the parking lot and recognized her small face behind
the wheel. It wasn't there; I called a taxi. By the time I got to
my house, it was one in the morning. I'd been traveling eleven
hours and was out more than $500. I stepped through the gate,
which creaked, and as if in answer, the light in the bedroom
went out, Bruno signaling that he was unavailable for a late-
night search party. As transparent as the ruse was, I still kept
my voice low. "Biscuit!" I called. "Biscuit!" I could hear the
despair in it. What creature in its right mind gravitates to despair? A Saint Bernard, maybe. But not a cat. At last I gave up
and went into the barn to sleep. Even with the heater on, it was

cold, and I lay under the thin blanket with my hands clasped between my thighs for warmth.

Back when I was in my thirties, it became common in certain circles to speak of love as discipline. I would characterize those circles as people made queasy by the sexual weightlessness of the preceding two decades, by *their* sexual weightlessness, people in bounding, caroming flight from the idea that love is never having to say you're sorry. Actually, the secret meaning of "love is discipline" might in fact be "I'm sorry." I'm sorry I didn't call you. I'm sorry I didn't show up. I'm sorry I came with somebody else. I'm sorry I lied about my wife, my husband, my girlfriend. I'm sorry I gave you that herpes. I'm sorry I forgot your birthday. I'm sorry I forgot the check. I'm sorry I told you I love you. At the time I meant it, I really did.

People spoke of commitments, and of those—usually, but not always, men—who avoided them as "Peter Pans" or "commitmentphobes." Suddenly, without any prompting, we had returned to the medicalized sexual ethics, or the moralizing sexual psychology, of the 1950s, when men—and back then it was always men—who didn't want to marry were diagnosed as immature or latent homosexuals, although in the 1950s homosexuality was itself seen as a kind of immaturity, as if every gay man were a little boy who hadn't yet learned what the different holes are for. By the time I am speaking of, however, a commitment didn't have to mean marriage; the sixties hadn't been entirely in vain. It was like medical insurance, with different plans offering different kinds of coverage. A commitment could mean that you no longer had sex with other people or that you wouldn't have sex with them without telling your partner first, so that she could then decide if the commitment was still working for her. It might be an agreement to see each other so many nights a week, to keep clothes and toiletries at each other's apartments, to spend the holidays with each other's families and buy presents for people who weren't related to you by blood or law. It might mean buying property together. It might mean maintaining this state of affairs until you finally decided to marry or found a reason why the commitment should be dissolved, the dissolution in a way being a fulfillment of the commitment, an escape clause written into it from the very start.

Of course, the idea of love as obligation is very old. It's one reason why we have marriage at all. In the beginning, it was obligation that made love possible, and that may still be so, going by studies that show that couples whose marriages were arranged report the same rate of happiness as those who chose their spouses. Having moved into this house of obligation, they make up their minds to be happy in it, although the windows are a little small and the kitchen doesn't have enough counter space. But obligations arise even in love that has no romantic component and even when there's no real reason to observe them. In the Bible, Ruth chooses to stay with her mother-in-law even after her husband dies, though it will mean a life of exile and poverty. "Whither thou goest, I will go," she tells Naomi. "And where thou lodgest, I will lodge" (Ruth 1:16). No rule is at stake. Ruth's husband is dead; she's free to go. Naomi has told her to go. Ruth begs to stay with her because she loves her. She has come to love her, love growing out of the old, otiose obligations like life bursting forth from something dead, as if a stone were suddenly to send forth green shoots. Love may arise out of obligations, but it also gives rise to them, and the latter kind are stronger than the mandates of any church or law court. We don't obey them out of fear but out of a murky inner necessity. We don't know why, only that if we don't, we won't be able to live with ourselves. "Law isn't all," goes a poem by Ishmael Reed:

> The driver's test
> says nothing
> about dogs, but people
> stop anyway.

I woke early, with an aching back. I shrugged on jeans and boots and went outside. The sky was the damp pale gray of a pearl. Dew hung on the grass, which needed mowing. When Rip Van Winkle returns to his house—the house he remembers leaving only the day before—he finds it "empty, forlorn, and apparently abandoned," and looking about me, I was struck by how decrepit my home had become, the grass too long, the screen door of the barn loose on its hinges. When I'd washed my face earlier, the water that came from the faucet had smelled of sulfur. I called for my cat in the same meek voice I had used five hours ago and then thought, Fuck it, it's my house, and shouted her name. "Biscuit!" Shouting, I made my way to the back of the garden and then through some brush that separated it from the college dorm where the year before

I'd seen a topless woman stride up the walk, purposefully but
without haste, her breasts bouncing.

After Rip learns of everything that has taken place during his
slumber—his wife and friends dead and his very country
transformed into this unprecedented thing, a republic—
Irving writes that his "heart passed away." He asks after Rip
Van Winkle, and his neighbors point to his son lounging by a
tree. "He doubted his own identity, and whether he was himself or another man." Alongside all his other losses, he has
lost his place in the world, the space that he alone occupied.
Such loss of place is a kind of death; it may be worse than the
physical kind. Thinking about our deaths, we imagine that
they will create a void in the lives of those who love us. The
thought of that void can be comforting, the way it can be
comforting to picture the weeping mourners at our funerals.
At least somebody is crying for us. But no one is crying for
Rip. No one seems to realize he's gone. His place in the
world has been filled, as if it had been dug not in earth but
the sea. "I'm not myself," he stammers. "I'm somebody else—
that's me yonder—no, that's somebody else; got into my
shoes—I was myself last night; but I fell asleep on the moun-
tain . . . and everything's changed, and I'm changed; and I
can't tell what's my name, or who I am!"

Another writer, one whose instincts were tragic rather than
comic, might have lingered on this trauma. Irving brushes it
aside. The displaced person is granted a new place in the
home of his daughter and the life of the village, where he takes

up his old occupation of lounging on the bench outside the inn. And although his voice falters when he asks after his wife, he takes the news of her death as "a drop of comfort." It's a heartless moment, but comedy is often heartless, and obligation doesn't always lead to love.

I felt something brush my ankle and looked down. It was Biscuit: that cat and no other. She grinned up at me, purring. I gaped down at her. When I reached for her, her small body felt as strong and supple as a trout's. Her fur was matted in places, and when I stroked her head, I encountered stiff quills of what might be tar or pine sap. "You dirty cat!" I scooped her up in my arms, and she let me press my face against her for a while before pushing me away. Once I let her down, she seemed to remember that she was angry with me: I'd left her. Ostentatiously, she turned her back, then went over to a shrub and sat down in its shade, her tail lashing. I didn't try to coax her out. I just watched her. I know that my feelings were absurd or at least inflated, just as I know that I have no knowledge, not even an inkling, of what Biscuit was actually feeling. She may have been irritated at being picked up and then mauled by a great, naked, bony human head. She may not even have remembered that I'd been gone. A cat is a wild thing whose nature has somehow grown around human beings and become entwined with theirs, but that nature is still wild.

After a while I got up—in my absorption I had sat down in the grass—and called to my cat before setting off toward the house. I didn't look back, but it was only a moment before she caught up with me. She stayed more or less at my side until we neared the driveway. Then she bounded ahead of me, pausing once to look back, or so it seemed to me, to make sure I was still there. Again, she grinned, openmouthed. When I opened the door of the house, she trotted inside as if she'd been gone no more than a few hours and was looking forward to taking a couple noisy mouthfuls of dry food, then curling up on her favorite chair.

In grade school science they taught us about the water cycle. Rain falls from the clouds and gathers in lakes and rivers and oceans, then evaporates in the heat of the sun to become water vapor, and the vapor rises to form new clouds, which release

rain once more. I still remember the poster, with its arrow-headed circle.

I'd like to think that love, too, is cyclical, at least under the right conditions.

The cycle begins with desire, the hot, quick spark that passes between two people and sets them ablaze. If it burns long enough, we call that love, and the people cleave together. They may not become one, a romantic fancy that has furnished the justification for a whole lot of pathology, but they fuse a little in spots, like tin soldiers cast in a single mold that have to be twisted apart. They pledge themselves, or as we've gotten used to saying, they commit, and even if their obligation remains informal, even if it remains unstated, they feel its rigor. Brought together by desire, they now sometimes resist it, the impulse to go home with the stranger at the art opening, to let the phone keep ringing while they watch college basketball or a crummy movie on the Lifetime channel. They obey desire's summons only when it leads them back to each other. That's how they stay together. Desire breeds love, which in turn breeds obligation, and the obligation makes love stronger.

But love is hot and obligation is cool, and below a certain temperature the fire goes out, and we look into the eyes in which we once saw a furnace and see only a stack of debts. Debt is another word for obligation. *Forgive us our debts, as we forgive our debtors.* The Gospels knew how hard it is to love someone who owes you something, or who you think does. It's even worse when you're the one who owes. Not even Jesus asked us to feel good about the bank. And so instead of being a self-renewing cycle, love may be more of a self-annihilating arc, canceled by what it calls into being. We build a chapel in the garden, and the next thing we know, the garden is filled with graves.

And yet a part of me protests: What about my cat? What made me look for her but obligation? If not for that, she might have starved or frozen to death.

Actually, I doubt it. When I came back north again that Christmas, I learned that Biscuit had made a second home in the dorm behind our house. That was probably where she'd disappeared to back in the fall. She'd go over and let the kids fuss over her and feed her canned tuna. F. once went looking for her and found her lying in a trance of pleasure on a girl's bed. When she picked Biscuit up to take her home, the cat struggled bitterly. She was the same with me. I gave her first crack at the canned food, even locking Wolfie, the gluttonous new male, in the bathroom so she could eat unmolested, but she took the privilege for granted, and when I tried to pet her, she jerked away. Day after day I courted her. She'd eat the food I set before her, snorting with greed and congestion. She might deign to let me stroke her. Then she'd leap onto the kitchen counter and crouch there, surveying the room. Sometimes I'd see her take me in. At such moments her gaze might soften a bit. It wasn't loving; at best you'd call it benign. And, really, it was no different from the gaze she turned on F. or the other cats (though in their case, her expression would also be a little gloating, since she was looking *down* at them) or the furniture, never for a moment doubting that all of it was hers.

11

BY THEN, F. HAD DECIDED SHE WANTED TO SEPARATE. It may be because she'd met somebody else. It may be because I'd run out of money and could barely pay my share of the bills, let alone the room tariff on a hotel in Rome. It may be because I'd yelled at her about leaving dirty dishes on the kitchen counter. It may be because I'd refused to take a stand against the landlord who'd left bags of garbage in the house we'd rented from him—not just refused but gone to the party his wife had thrown for his birthday the previous summer and, I believe, brought along a present, though not an expensive one. It may be because I'd threatened to stuff Wilfredo into the car and take him down to the city and drop him on his mother's doorstep at two in the morning, and it may be because of the expression F. saw on my face as I said this. It was not formed to excite passion.

"Their life is mysterious, it is like a forest," Salter writes of his married couple. "From far off it seems a unity, it can be comprehended, described, but closer it begins to separate, to break into light and shadow, the density blinds one."

My problem is that I can write only from inside the forest.

F. came down to North Carolina to tell me. We took a walk along the beach. Winters in that part of the country start later than they do up north and they're a lot milder, but it was cold enough, a day or two after Thanksgiving, that we walked with our shoulders hunched, our hands clenched in our pockets. When we faced into the wind, our eyes watered. I can't reconstruct the conversation, except that at some point she asked me, "Do you want to know what I felt then?" and I said I didn't want to know. It was probably the first time in all the years we'd been together that I didn't want to know what she was feeling, or had felt. I didn't want to look at her, and this too was new to me. I was angry but not in a way that can be assuaged by yelling, and so it seemed to me that my only recourse was to seal myself against her—and also to refrain from bursting out at her, to refrain especially from asking her not to leave. She could do what she wanted. The image that comes to mind is of a stone figure, eyeless, earless, noseless, mouthless, without any of the apertures that allow one human being to be penetrated by another, or rather by a sense impression of that other, as it may be made by the light reflecting off her person or by the molecules of air set in motion by her voice or the ones that bear the chemical signatures of her body. I suppose what I'm thinking of is one of the human beings who were petrified by the volcanic ash that spewed from Mt. Vesuvius when it erupted in AD 79, destroying the city of Pompeii. The date of

that catastrophe is traditionally given as August 24, but archaeological studies suggest it really took place three months later,
at the end of November.

In view of our conversation, why did F. then invite me to come
up for Christmas? Why did I agree to come? It was in many
ways like other Christmases we'd spent together. We bought a
tree and hung it with lights, tinsel, and ornaments her family
had given her, including a ponderous angel made from an iron
cowbell I half blamed for causing an earlier tree of ours to tip
over. At the time I was in another room, so all I heard was a terrifying crash and F.'s even more terrifying shriek, and when I
ran in, she was unhurt and laughing helplessly at the felled
tree and scattered ornaments. Amazingly, only a few of them
were broken. The cowbell, of course, was intact.

We gave each other gifts. We went to some Christmas parties, where we behaved like any other couple, and at times
even a loving one, though perhaps a couple who have something uncomfortable pending between them, as if they'd been
fighting when they left the house and are wondering if they'll
start up again when they get home. On Christmas Eve, we
flipped through the channels to see if any of them was showing
A Christmas Carol, the old one with Alistair Sim as Scrooge.
We couldn't find it, only a bunch of newer *Carols* starring con-
temporary actors and shot in color that browbeat the eye. We'd
done the same thing the Christmas before and the Christmas
before that, and almost all the Christmases we'd spent together
except for the one time we had the initiative to rent the movie,
which you could only get on tape. We groused about a world

that wouldn't let you see Dickens's characters in the somber black-and-white of Victorian mourning, on degraded footage whose tiny, writhing imperfections might be homunculi of the ghosts Marley shows Scrooge outside his window. We wanted to see the Scrooge of our childhood, and they wouldn't give it to us, and it was cruddy.

A little after New Year's, I flew back down south, with the expectation that the next time I came back up, it would be to pack my things and move to a new home. For a long time afterward, we had little contact. In April, F. wrote me saying she wanted to see if we could still be together. I read her letter in haste, then again slowly, with silent snorts of incredulity. It held no conventional expression of longing or regret; at times she seemed to be scolding me. On one level, I would have liked F. to say how wonderful I was and how awful she'd been, but I would have been suspicious if she had. I was suspicious anyway. Still it occurred to me that she was presenting herself to me the same way she had when we were sitting across from each other in a tea shop ten years before: bluntly, without apology, revealing herself and then withdrawing, inviting my compassion—maybe even my tenderness—but at any moment ready to repel it. She was letting me see her in the fullness of her being. In the end, I wrote back not because I wanted to be with her but because she had made me curious. Of course I know what they say about curiosity and cats. But I'm not a cat. I've only loved a few.

In the months after I came back, we went to see a therapist who had only one eye. At our first session, she told us she'd lost the other one to cancer. My guess is she did that so that we

wouldn't be distracted by macabre curiosity as to why one lens of her glasses was completely opaque. She had us play with little toys, which was embarrassing but also kind of fun, though not enough fun for us to pay $75 an hour for it, which was why in the end we stopped seeing her.

After an especially bitter fight over the Labor Day weekend, F.'s chest and back erupted in raised red marks. She thought they might be a spider bite. She's deathly afraid of spiders, and although the marks weren't especially painful, the unease they inspired in her kept mounting until, finally, while we were at the county fare watching the equestrian events, she said she wanted to go to the medical trailer. The trailer was manned by a male health aide who must have weighed four hundred pounds. His mass seemed to fill every inch of the cabin. It threatened to ooze out the windows like dough extruded from a malfunctioning bread mixer, not a home model but the commercial kind,

with a drum a child could stand in. There was barely room for
F. to step inside and show him her welts. The aide, who had
probably been hired to care for fairgoers laid low by overeating
or motion-sick from riding the Fireball, took a look at F.'s marks
and said they were above his pay grade.

We walked through the heat and dust to our car. Along with
being worried about F., I felt nostalgic. Our first house had
been next door to the fairground's rear entrance, and at night
we'd been buffeted by the clatter of the rides and the thump
and twang of country and western bands that I referred to col-
lectively as the Haylofters; F. laughed every time I said it. We
drove to the emergency room of our local hospital, the same
one she'd been taken to years before when Bitey had made her
dislocate her arm. Strictly speaking, it wasn't the same ER,
since the hospital had been renovated. A bored triage nurse
had F. pull up her shirt and fill out some insurance forms,
then sent us back into the empty lobby. The procedure took
no more than three minutes. After we'd been waiting another
fifteen or twenty, we were joined by a family steering a young
quadriplegic man in an enormous whirring black wheelchair.
It seemed not only to be carrying him but assisting with his
vital functions, perhaps even making his heart beat. Whatever
was wrong with him was probably more serious than a spider
bite, but he and his people were also made to wait, and about
a half hour later, F. decided she wanted to go home. The next
day she saw her dermatologist, who told her she had shingles.
They're often brought on by stress, and hers went away after a
course of Acyclovir. A few months later, the hospital sent us a
bill for $400.

There were more fights. These weren't so much ugly as petty. I don't remember ever calling F. a name or her calling me one, but sometimes I imagined a cartoon in which I chased her around the dining table, kicking her in the butt. The kicks would be deeply embarrassing to her but not painful. Once, she told me, not in the cartoon but in real life, she fantasized about my being killed in a car wreck and telling friends she was too distraught to make funeral arrangements: they could bury me if they wanted. Once during a phone call, we both blurted out that we wanted to be done with the marriage, seemingly in the same breath and in the same words. I remember staring down at the receiver as if it had bitten me, or she had bitten me through it. Whose teeth had made those marks?

Sometime during this period, I told F. I wanted to stay to-gether. Looking back, I can say I based my decision on the tiny psychic adjustments that took place as we crouched on the shrink's floor, arranging tiny dinosaurs and armored warriors. I made it because of what I'd felt when F. showed me the welts on her body, which looked like they'd been made by a red-hot wire: I mean a horror and pity so pressing that I instantly forgot what we'd been fighting about and for the next several hours thought of little more than making sure she was taken care of; we had plenty of time to fight some more once I knew she was all right. Maybe I just liked having a partner who laughed when I griped about the Haylofters.

If only, on hearing me say I wanted her, F. had thrown her-self in my arms and said she was so happy, she wanted me too. If only she'd wept with gratitude or relief. She didn't. It's prob-ably not in her nature. But her response felt grudging to me; it still feels grudging, and so I am not content. She makes demands; she bitches at me and complains that I bitch at her. Sometimes I wish I'd kicked her out of that car in Rome. *Va al diavolo!* Sometimes I think that with improved employment opportunities and convenient packaged foods, men and women no longer need each other enough to stay together out of stoicism or habit. They have to choose, not just once, but again and again, a day, an hour, a minute at a time. When a choice has to be repeated so often, it falls subject to the same odds that govern the tossing of a coin. Sooner or later, the choice will be no. And sometimes I think that F. and I are like two plodding amateur dancers who take what they expect will be a short, heavy-footed leap—not even a leap but a jump—and discover that they are floating three feet above the ground. It's only when they look down that they fall.

In the months to come, we'll move to yet another house, a very nice one, overlooking a pond where muskrats swim tirelessly back and forth and a blue heron sometimes skims across the water looking, in elongated profile, like a hieroglyph come to life. The cats watch, fascinated, from a distance. They like to prowl the reeds in search of things to kill, but they know they're not the equal of a blue heron.

You'd think we could find peace in a place this beautiful, but we cannot. Both of us are waiting for something to happen.

Today we fought again, I forget what about. Needing to get away from F., I stepped onto the front porch, leaving the door half-open behind me. It's spring, the days are lengthening, and although it was closing on evening, the sky was still bright. Light fell slanting onto the grass. At the foot of the porch steps,

Biscuit was crouching, her neck craned forward, her shoulders hunched. Every cell of her being was straining toward something. It took me a while to see what it was. About fifty feet away, beside the tool shed, were two rabbits. They stood some ten feet apart on their hind legs, their soft plump muzzles working as they nibbled. Rabbits always seem to be nibbling something—carrots, cabbages, clover. I had no idea what these rabbits were chowing down on, but everything about them, down to the angle of their ears, seemed to express the tension between appetite and caution. Even as they ate, they kept watch about them with their depthless black eyes.

They must have seen Biscuit, just as she plainly saw them. And although I'm always conscious that my judgments about what a cat is thinking or feeling aren't really judgments but projections, at that moment I was pretty confident about what Biscuit was thinking. She was trying to decide which rabbit to go for. She knew she couldn't get them both. And the rabbits were waiting to see which of them she'd go for, though I suspect they also knew she couldn't get either of them: they were too far from her, and if they'd seen Biscuit in action, they'd know she isn't the fastest cat. Her poor legs are too short. Biscuit was watching the rabbits. The rabbits were watching Biscuit. I was watching them all. I was the fourth element in this constellation of viewers, the biggest and slowest moving, and the only one, to our knowledge, possessed of powers of self-reflection. Of the four beings that had come together in this space, I was the one that watched itself watching the others, in effect adding a fifth element to the arrangement, an ethereal spectatorial self that floated above the porch, insatiable in its watchfulness. This trait may be what makes me a less effective predator than Biscuit. I'm pretty confident that if I were shrunk down to their size, I'd be a less successful prey animal than the rabbits.

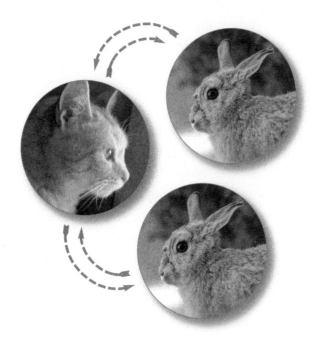

I stood like this for what felt like a very long time, savoring the perfection of the moment, for as moments go, it was perfect. Then, very slowly, I sidled to the door and leaned inside. F. was sitting at the dining table. She looked exactly like herself, that woman and no other. I motioned to her; she came to me. Keeping my voice low, I told her, "Come and see," and I pointed out the door to where the cat crouched watching the rabbits and the rabbits stood watching the cat.

ACKNOWLEDGMENTS

THIS BOOK HAD FOUR EARLY READERS, WHO WERE GENEROUS enough to look at its chapters virtually as I wrote them and tell me what they thought: Rebecca Chace, Erin Clermont, Sheila Keenan, and Corinne Manning. If not for them, I might have abandoned this project. I also thank Jo Ann Beard, Annie Bellerose, Clyde Edgerton, Mark Irwin, Tracy O'Neill, and Carmen Rodriguez, Michael White, and Marci Vogel for reading portions of the work at different times. My gratitude to Renee Sedliar, my editor at Da Capo, and my agent Gillian Mackenzie and her assistant Adriann Ranta for their faith and well-placed doubts. Thanks also to Cisca Schreefel, Jennifer Kelland, Linda Mark, and Jonathan Sainsbury for turning the manuscript into a book, and to Lissa Warren and Sean Maher for publicizing it. Special acknowledgments go to Chris Noland of the Black Cat Fireworks Company, Christina Campbell, and the magnificent Martha Ciattei for furnishing photographs and artwork. Extraordinary thanks to Jesse McCloskey for his original drawings. You can see his paintings at the Claire Oliver Gallery.

Jeanne-Marie Laskas, Donald Bialostosky, and my new colleagues at the University of Pittsburgh offered me an intellectual and professional home after many years of nomadism. I'm also grateful to my teaching cohorts at the University of North Carolina at Wilmington, Bard College, the City College of New York, St. Mary's College of California, the Iowa Summer Writers' Festival, and Ashland University, especially Marilyn Abildskov, Karen Bender, Sladja Blazan, David Buuck, Peter Campion, Stephen Cope, Philip Gerard, Carmen Gimenez Smith, Kythe Heller, Rebecca Lee, Joe Mackall, Amy Margolis, Miranda Melis, Marie Regan, Joan Retallack, Robert Siegel, Eleni Stecopoulos, Frederic Tuten, Michael White, and David Wolach.

My gratitude to the John Simon Guggenheim Memorial Foundation and the Richard D. and Mary Jane Edwards Endowed Publication Fund for their support, as well as to the Rockefeller Foundation and the Bellagio Center.

I thank the people who at different times cared for my cats: Jo Ann Beard and Scott Spencer, Heather Dini, Carolina Gonzalez Hutton, Litia Perta, Sheri Sceroler, and the doctors and staff of Rhinebeck Animal Hospital.

My final thanks go to Ellen Trachtenberg and Mary Gaitskill, for reasons they know.

Peter Trachtenberg
May 22, 2012

NOTES

Chapter 1

8   **A "prey-like" moving dummy:** Patrick Bateson, "Behavioural Development in the Cat," in *The Domestic Cat: The Biology of Its Behaviour*, ed. Dennis C. Turner and Patrick Bateson, 2nd ed. (Cambridge: Cambridge University Press, 2000), 17.

12 *And Juan was mad about her*: James Salter, *Light Years* (San Francisco: North Point Press, 1982), 87.

14 **"They were so miserable":** Ibid., 125.

15 **"Like a master or an illness":** Marcel Proust, *Swann's Way*, trans. C. K. Scott Moncrieff and Terence Kilmartin (New York: Random House, 1981), 249–250.

Chapter 2

27 **"To approach the soul":** Marcel Proust, *Within a Budding Grove*, trans. C. K. Moncrieff and Terence Kilmartin (New York: Random House, 1981), 1009.

31 **Versus 80 for nonbreeding "subordinates":** Olof Liberg et al., "Density, Spatial Organization and Reproductive

Tactics in the Domestic Cat and Other Felids," in Turner and Bateson, *The Domestic Cat*, 126.

33 **"Out of the puddly concupiscence of the flesh"**: Augustine of Hippo, *Confessions*, trans. Albert Cook Outler (Philadelphia: Westminster Press, 1955), bk. II, ch. 2.

37 **"You are emptying the world so we can be alone"**: Frank O'Hara, "Now That I Am in Madrid and Can Think," *The Selected Poems of Frank O'Hara* (New York: Vintage Books, 1974), 174–175.

42 **"Because it was forbidden"**: Augustine of Hippo, *Confessions*, trans. J. G. Pilkington (Edinburgh: T & T Clark, 1876), bk. II, ch. 4, 30.

Chapter 3

62 **"Under the same terms"**: Theodore Evergates, ed. and trans., *Feudal Society in Medieval France: Documents from the County of Champagne* (Philadelphia: University of Pennsylvania Press, 1993), 41–42.

63 **"To the day of my death"**: Philippe Ariès, "The Indissoluble Marriage," in *Western Sexuality: Practice and Precept in Past and Present Times*, ed. Philippe Ariès and André Béjin (Oxford: Basil Blackwell, 1985), 151–152.

63 **"Marriage is established"**: Cited in Conor McCarthy, *Marriage in Medieval England: Law, Literature, and Practice* (Melton, UK: Boydell Press, 2004), 22.

64 **Fourteen out of seventeen theologians said she could:** Jean-Louis Flandrin, "Sex in Married Life in the Early Middle Ages: The Church's Teaching and Behavioural Reality," in Ariès and Béjin, *Western Sexuality*, 119.

72 **"When he is thrown from a high place"**: Dorothy Hartley,

trans., *Lost Country Life* (New York: Pantheon, 1979). Available online at http://www.godecookery.com/mtales /mtales07.htm.

73 **"As patient as a cat whose paws are being grilled"**: Robert Darnton, *The Great Cat Massacre and Other Episodes in French Cultural History* (New York: Basic Books, 1984), 83, 90–91.

75 **A "deputy kitten"**: Cited in B. Mike Fitzgerald and Dennis C. Turner, "Hunting Behavior of Domestic Cats and Their Impact on Prey Populations," in Turner and Bateson, *The Domestic Cat*, 155.

Chapter 4

81 **"To draw attention to it"**: Augustine of Hippo, *Confessions*, trans. Henry Chadwick (Oxford: Oxford University Press, 1991), bk. I, ch. viii, 11.

81 **John Bradshaw and Charlotte Cameron-Beaumont identify some of these below:** John Bradshaw and Charlotte Cameron-Beaumont, "The Signalling Repertoire of the Domestic Cat and Its Undomesticated Relatives," in Turner and Bateson, *The Domestic Cat*, 71 (simplified by the author).

92 **Cats performed worse than pigeons:** Patrick Bateson and Dennis C. Turner, "Postscript: Questions About Cats," in Turner and Bateson, *The Domestic Cat*, 236.

94 **"The impulse leading to the successful movement"**: E. L. Thorndike, "Animal Intelligence: An Experimental Study of the Associative Processes in Animals," *Psychological Review* 2, no. 4, Monograph Supplements No. 8 (New York: MacMillan, 1898).

95 **They began staying longer:** Carlos A. Driscoll et al., "The Near Eastern Origin of the Desert Cat," *Science* (July 27, 2007): 317, 519–522.

95 **"Escapes by his dallying":** Christopher Smart, "Jubilate Agno." Available online at http://www.poets.org/viewmedia .php/prmMID/15798.

96 **Five feline Eves:** Driscoll et al., "The Near Eastern Origin of the Desert Cat."

98 **Called attention to it as an individual:** J. D. Vigne et al. "Early Taming of the Cat in Cyprus," *Science* (April 9, 2004): 304.

100 **"Our mental photographs of it are always blurred":** Proust, *Within a Budding Grove*, 528.

107 **"As having originated in ourselves":** Ibid., 655.

111 **"Or lover of wisdom":** Plato, *Symposium*, trans. Benjamin Jowett, The Internet Classics Archive, http://classics.mit .edu/Plato/symposium.html.

111 **"Even for a moment":** Ibid.

112 **"Is called love":** Plato, *Phaedrus*, trans. Benjamin Jowett, Greece.com, http://www.greece.com/library/plato/phaedrus _01.html.

113 **"But was afraid to be free of it":** Augustine, *Confessions*, trans., Henry Chadwick, 107.

113 **"With the bodily senses":** Ibid., 62.

113 **Is mere indigence:** Ibid., 278.

115 **"As unstable as a dream":** Proust, *Within a Budding Grove*, 631.

Chapter 5

143 **"After the rest of it had gone":** Lewis Carroll, *Alice's Adventures in Wonderland*, ch. VI, Carnegie Mellon School

of Computer Science, http://www.cs.cmu.edu/~rgs/alice-VI.html.

145 **"To take (in the widest applications)"**: http://scripturetext.com/genesis/20-2.htm.

151 **He feels ashamed:** Jacques Derrida, *The Animal That Therefore I Am*, ed. Marie-Louise Mallet, trans. David Wills (New York: Fordham, 2008), 3–11.37.

163 **"But the indenture of a man"**: Plato, *Symposium.*

Chapter 6

174 **"They are mourning the dead"**: Peter Metcalfe and Richard Huntington, *Celebrations of Death: The Anthropology of Mortuary Ritual*, 2nd ed. (Cambridge: Cambridge University Press, 1991), 55.

175 **"Because at this point the Maestro died"**: John Rizzo, "Why Didn't Puccini Finish *Turandot?*," Italian Opera Company of Chicago, http://italianoperachicago.com/interior/Articles/Verdi/Why%20didn%27t%20Puccini%20finish%20Turandot.htm.

Chapter 7

194 **"Paler than / dry grass"**: Sappho, "Fragment," in *Sappho: A New Translation*, trans. Mary Barnard (1958; rpt. Berkeley: University of California Press, 1999), 39.

195 **We never met again:** Gerald Stern, "Another Insane Devotion," in *Early Collected Poems: 1965–1992* (New York: Norton, 2010), 386.

Chapter 8

217 **"That crowd around it"**: John Ruskin, *Modern Painters,*

Part III (1856; rpt. Whitefish, MT: Kessinger Publishing, 2005), 151.

217　"**Where men fall and rise not again**": Quoted by Phyllis Rose, *Parallel Lives: Five Victorian Marriages* (New York: Alfred A. Knopf, 1984), 54.

218　"**Not formed to excite passion**": Ibid., 55.

218　"**He was disgusted with my person**": Vanessa Thorpe, "What Was John Ruskin Thinking on His Unhappy Wedding Night?," *The Observer*, March 13, 2010, http://www .guardian.co.uk/film/2010/mar/14/john-ruskin-wedding -effie-gray.

231　"**Smeared out in equal parts**": Erwin Schrödinger, "Die gegenwärtige Situation in der Quantenmechanik [The Present Situation in Quantum Mechanics]," *Naturwissenschaften* (November 1935). Cited at http://www.phobe .com/s_cat/s_cat.html.

232　"**That makes one cling to a woman**": Salter, *Light Years*, 205.

232　"**It cannot be regained**": Ibid., 205.

Chapter 9

239　**How did she know it would work?**: The extent to which cats consciously manipulate their owners calls for further research. In 2009, scientists at the University of Sussex discovered that cats use different purrs to solicit food and express pleasure: the former contain a high-frequency component similar to that found in the cry of a human baby. Humans who listened to recordings described the solicitation purrs as more urgent than the other kind and less pleasant. Karen McComb et al., "The Cry Embedded

Within the Purr," *Current Biology* 19, no. 13 (July 14, 2009): 507–508.

241 **"That belongs to the rat family"**: Mauny de Mornay, *Livre d'eleveur et du proprietaire d'animaux domestiques* (Paris: A. L. Pagnerre etc., Editeurs, 1837), 287. Facsimile edition available at http://books.google.com/books?printsec=front cover&dq=intitle:%22animaux+domestiques%22&lr=&as _drrb_is=b&as_minm_is=0&as_miny_is=1800&as_maxm _is=0&as_maxy_is=1880&cd=36&pg=PA287&id=tBkG wxXqxpgC&num=100&as_brr=1#v=onepage&q&f=false.

Chapter 10

255 **"But people / stop anyway"**: Ishmael Reed, "Untitled," in *New and Collected Poems*, 1964–2007 (New York: Thunder's Mouth, 2007), 131.

255 **"And apparently abandoned"**: Washington Irving, *Rip Van Winkle and Other Selected Stories* (New York: Tor, 1993), 7. Available at http://www.bartleby.com/195/4.html.

256 **"Whether he was himself or another man"**: Ibid., 8.

256 **"I can't tell what's my name, or who I am!"**: Ibid., 8.

Chapter 11

264 **"The density blinds one"**: Salter, *Light Years*, 23.

PHOTO CREDITS